AMAZON BOOM 2020

Sophie Howard

Copyright © Sophie Howard

No part of this publication may be reproduced, stored in a retrieval system, or transmitted in any form or by any means, electronic, mechanical, photocopying, recording, or otherwise, without written permission of the publisher.

AMAZON BOOM

Could You Make A Side Income Selling Products On Amazon - Without Leaving Your Home? by Sophie Howard

Publisher: Blue Sky Amazon Publishing in partnership with Knowledge Source

© 2020 All rights reserved. www.blueskyamazon.com

For general information on our products and services, please contact support@knowledgesource.com.au

This digital book contains general education about starting an e-commerce business on Amazon. For specialized accounting, tax, legal, or financial advice, please see a qualified professional.

All businesses offer potential loss of money as well as the opportunity for gain, and no guarantee of income is express or implied. Results shared are not typical, just examples of what others have achieved. As in all businesses, different people will have different results depending on a variety of factors such as past experience, skill level etc.

TABLE OF CONTENTS

AN INTRODUCTION TO AMAZON 1

Take Control of Your Life and Your Lifestyle 4

How do you manage your OWN Amazon empire? 7

How much money can you expect to make from
an Amazon business? 11

Who Can Succeed at Amazon? 12

Building Your Empire from the Products First! 19

What is AMAZON Today and How Could It Make Me Cashflow? 23

A little bit about Jeff and how he makes me serious money 26

How to Put Your Amazon Business on Autopilot 33

How to Find Winning Products to Sell on Amazon 39

How to find the hottest products 48

What's Your First Step to Building Your Global Amazon Empire? 50

HOW AMAZON THINKS 52

Meet Jeff 53

The Everything Store 54

Partner with #1 56

Amazon Gets the Edge 58

The Benefits of Amazon FBA 60

Global Domination 61

100% Customer Focus 63

Play by the Rules 65

Do the Right Thing 69

COMMON MISTAKES MADE BY AMAZON SELLERS   **71**

Mistake 1: Getting started 76

Mistake 2: Looking for "the One" 79

Mistake 3: In Software we Trust? 85

Mistake 4: Bright Shiny Objects 93

Mistake 5: Is Facebook Really Your Friend? 97

Summary of the 5 mistakes to avoid 102

AN INTERVIEW WITH SOPHIE HOWARD
SUCCESSFUL AMAZON SELLER   **104**

How a Busy Mum of 2 Cracked 7 Figures on
Amazon An Interview with Sophie Howard 104

100 HOT AMAZON PRODUCTS   **126**

Art, sewing and crafts 127

Beauty and Personal Care 132

Industrial and Scientific 137

Patio Lawn and Garden 142

Toys and Games 148

Tools and Home Improvement 153

Sports and Outdoor 159

Kitchen and Dining 164

Grocery and Gourmet 169

Health and Household 174

QUESTIONS AND ANSWERS WITH THE AMAZON EXPERT
SOPHIE HOWARD   **180**

WHAT OTHER PEOPLE ARE SAYING ABOUT SOPHIE HOWARD   **201**

SELLING AN AMAZON BUSINESS FOR A BIG POTENTIAL PAYDAY   **213**

FAST-START ONLINE MASTERCLASS

HOT SELLING AMAZON PRODUCTS
AND HOW TO FIND THEM

CLICK HERE TO REGISTER NOW

CHAPTER ONE

AN INTRODUCTION TO AMAZON

Hi, I'm Sophie Howard.

If you want to learn about how to make a healthy income selling on Amazon then you're in the right place.

In this book, I'm going to teach you all about Amazon. I have created millions of dollars in sales in my businesses, and I am going to teach you how you could potentially build a successful ecommerce business using Amazon.

Amazon has revolutionized consumer buying habits across the globe. Today, without doubt, Amazon is the dominant force in retail.

Hundreds of millions of people use Amazon on a daily basis by either spending money on Amazon, or making money from Amazon. It's really that simple.

I don't know about you, but I much prefer MAKING money

from Amazon, and I'm sure you will too. And that's the focus of this book: How to create potentially massive income streams that will give you the freedom and financial security to live the life you want.

In this book I share all I have learned about building a successful business on Amazon. I share all my top tips for making sure your Amazon journey is both successful, stress-free and enjoyable.

Please note my results are not typical but I want to share with you what I've learned to give you the maximum chance of success.

So, buckle up and let's get started.

I was at work....

I opened the message.

It was a beautiful photo of my kids on a gorgeous sunny weekday morning. There they are happily playing, enjoying the fresh air and warm weather. It made me smile. And then I realized, in that instant, that I was missing out on all these wonderful precious times with my children. The lovely nanny got to spend time with my children instead of me! I realized that if nothing changed, I was going to miss out on all those special years with the kids.

This is the actual photo that gave me the push I needed to make that change. It helped me decide that it was time to do something differently, very differently.

The more I thought about it, the more I realized that, not only was I missing out on all the precious time with my children, I wasn't really getting ahead financially either, despite all that effort.

I was also working part-time hours but was delivering a full-time workload in those hours.

Does this sound familiar?

In that instant I knew it was time to explore something different; a different way of making a living. I wanted financial freedom AND the ability to be at home with my kids. I knew that I had to find a way to get out of the nine-to-five grind.

Even though I didn't know WHAT I was going to do or know HOW I was going to do it. I just knew that I was going to figure something out.

For people who've made the transition from being a full-time employee to full- time entrepreneur, there's been a moment like that. It was truly a light bulb moment.

That was my light bulb moment, and I knew I had to act quickly. I had made the decision to change, and I knew that if I wanted the future to be different, I had to do something different immediately. I started to explore my options, see what opportunities were available to me. I started to make my plan.

During this transition phase, I held onto my day job whilst I worked on my plan for the future. This gave me some short-term security whilst I built new skills and explored new ways of generating income. I held on to the day job whilst I laid the foundations of my new business, and then eventually I got to write the best (and the last) letter to my manager.....

Dear Boss, I quit. Love Sophie.

And suddenly there I was. I was out on my own, and I knew that I had to make it work! It was exciting, and at times unnerving, but I was committed to building something new, and a something that was going to work for me.

I knew that it wasn't always going to be smooth sailing (nothing ever is), but I was motivated, committed and very excited at the future I was about to build for myself, and my family.

TAKE CONTROL OF YOUR LIFE AND YOUR LIFESTYLE

My plan was clear: I wanted out of the day job. I wanted to build a sustainable business that would work for me and provide security for my family.

Choosing to quit my day job and committing to starting something completely new was not a decision that was taken lightly. There was a lot of planning involved during that transition period. This was the path that I had chosen, but I appreciate that not everyone has the appetite for such dramatic change.

Does that mean that opportunities are not open to you if you choose to keep the day job whilst generating a second income?

Absolutely not! Opportunity is everywhere. Most people choose to keep their day jobs in the short term, and that's absolutely fine. In fact, the wonderful thing about developing a second income stream with an Amazon business is that it is possible to establish, develop and grow an Amazon business in just half an hour or an hour of your day everyday.

Even with minimal time input, it is possible that your business can actually become sizable and profitable. There is no ceiling with an Amazon business. It is perfectly feasible keep the day job whilst starting an Amazon business.

I chose to take a different route: I wanted out of the day job completely. That was my motivation. I spent a lot of time researching my options, and I considered many different kinds of businesses. And then I came across Amazon.

There are a multitude of things to love about an Amazon business, and I'll cover these a little later in this book. But, once I understood Amazon, I got started straight away. I established my business and got selling successfully on Amazon quickly.

Did I make mistakes? Absolutely!

But I was committed to learning and finding better ways of doing things. I tested different ways of selling, different products, and I gradually got better and better at it. I was efficient and selling successfully. The extra income I was generating enabled me to make some really big lifestyle changes.

Imagine you're earning an additional two thousand or eight thousand or fifteen thousand dollars per month thanks to your Amazon business. That level of income generation from an Amazon business is entirely possible. A small selection of good products selling online using Amazon as a sales platform is completely achievable.

What would that extra income mean for you? What would you do differently?

What would you change in your life if you had that extra income? Let me ask you a question:

What did my extra Amazon income mean for me?

My extra Amazon income enabled me to increase savings:

I was able to start saving large sums of money. When I worked the 9-5 day job, I was just making ends meet. I certainly wasn't putting savings aside. The extra income from my Amazon business enabled me to start saving money.

- **My extra Amazon income enabled me to pay off the mortgage faster:**

    Nobody likes giving the bank all the compound interest that accumulates over thirty years lifespan of a home loan. The extra income generated from my Amazon businesses helped me to pay down my mortgage quicker.

- **My extra Amazon income enabled me to pay off the mortgage completely!**

    Not only was I able to pay down my mortgage quicker, I was actually able to clear my mortgage completely with the sale of my first and second Amazon businesses, not only once but TWICE. I am so proud that I was able to do that in my thirties. I am so proud that I have cleared all my debts and secured my family's financial future.

SOPHIE HOWARD

HOW DO YOU MANAGE YOUR OWN AMAZON EMPIRE?

Amazon has the potential to generate a lot of income, and you actually don't need to give up the day job to do that.

Selling on Amazon is an online business. Once established, all that is needed is a stable Wi-Fi connection to run it.

The process for starting an Amazon business is quick and straight forward. There are no big time or financial commitments to get started.

Because it's online, I can run my Amazon business from any where. I run my mine from the kitchen table in New Zealand! From there I am able to access millions of customers worldwide. I sell on Amazon in the States, the UK, Europe and now Australia as Amazon has started there. None of my customers are in New Zealand.

As well as being convenient, an Amazon business can be very lean and time efficient. Once established, it takes about thirty to sixty minutes a day to run. That means that, if you choose not to, you don't need to give up your day job while you are getting started.

If you want to know about how to become a successful Amazon seller, then you're in the right place.

In this book, I'll assume you know nothing about Amazon. We'll start at the very beginning, and I'll take you through the process of getting started and selling successfully online

Buckets and Pipelines

Once you understand Buckets and Pipelines, you'll never look at your day job in the same way again.

Just before we really get into Amazon, there's one thing I want to cover briefly; the concept of how we earn our money.

For convenience, I'm going to assume you're in some sort of day job. I'm also going to assume that you are keen to replace your income or supplement your income.

Having a job and a career is great. It can be professionally fulfilling, and at the end of every month we receive a paycheck. But when we go to work, we trade our time for money (a salary or an hourly rate). We have to work every hour, even if we've got a high-performance job in the city; we may be commanding a high hourly rate or bringing home a great salary.

BUT, as soon as we stop working, we stop earning.

Our employers give us a standard number of weeks off per year with annual leave and paid holidays. So, we're committed and tied to commuting into work, day in day out. We must keep turning up to work and working every dollar we earn.

Let's compare that analogy to getting water down at a village…

…Imagine that in the village, a couple of guys, Bill and Ben, have to go and carry buckets to bring water back to their village. They do that every day. But, if Bill and Ben ever stop carrying the buckets, then there's suddenly no water in the village. The same applies to when we go to work: day in day out, we travel to our day jobs and bring home a paycheck. The moment we stop going to work, the paychecks also stop. So we're tied.

Now imagine that Bill, who is the smarter of the two, starts to dig a hole one day.

Everybody's a bit baffled about what he's doing.

It doesn't seem to make any sense.

He should be really tired from carrying his buckets, but he continues digging his hole. Next, he digs a big trench, and then he put some pipes down. A few days later he connects all the pipes together. He then turns on the tap and watches the water flow continuously to the village (and then he probably pours himself a cocktail and collapses into a hammock).

Bill has built a steady stream of water that flows to his village consistently. He's built a pipeline and, whenever he needs to, he can just turn the tap on to provide water to the village. He no longer needs to carry buckets.

When you apply this concept to how you earn money, things get interesting. There's a fundamental difference between a pipeline business and a bucket business. The concept also extends beyond business to your lifestyle.

Most people have 'bucket' lives.

As employees, they are simply "carrying buckets", day in day out. This is hard work, it's relentless, and it's an inefficient use of time. In contrast, a pipeline business is efficient because it brings the cash to you, rather than you having to go out and collect it every day.

In a nutshell, that's the secret of the wealthy.

Building a pipeline business enables you to escape the trap of "hours for dollars".

When I was looking to start a business and I was at home with a baby and a toddler, I was keen to make sure that this wasn't going to be something that created another fifty hours of work that I had to do from home. Whatever business I chose had to be leveraged and scalable. It wasn't to be me doing every hour of work just to keep things afloat.

I also knew that I didn't want to have a time intensive products business where I would find myself at the post office everyday, sending individual parcels and packages out to customers. I also knew that didn't want to have to spend time on client phone calls and customer service.

I knew I needed to build a business that could be run on autopilot to some degree.

That's when I worked out that Amazon was going to be a good fit for me.

Understanding the difference between a bucket business and a pipeline business is a crucial. You can carry endless buckets in a day-job or you can choose to build a cash flow pipeline which will give you control of your time and give you a way out from the "hours for dollars" trap

That's really the secret of the wealthy and the secret to creating a consistent efficient passive income stream.

HOW MUCH MONEY CAN YOU EXPECT TO MAKE FROM AN AMAZON BUSINESS?

According to Amazon CEO Jeff Bezos, there are more than 140,000 people who've built pipeline businesses on Amazon who make more than a **hundred thousand US dollars a year in sales on Amazon**.

That's a really significant number of people who are generating great revenue from their Amazon sales businesses.

Importantly, most of those people are not techy whiz kids with multi-million- dollar businesses, glamorously flying around the world sourcing products to sell on Amazon.

More often, these are usually people who still hold a day job in a city or a large regional town, around the world. These people are stay at home moms and dads, people with other commitments. An increasing number of these people are retirees. There are also young people building great pipeline businesses on Amazon to support themselves through university and college. There is a huge mix of people selling products successfully in Amazon.

For this diverse mix of sellers, Amazon represents a fantastic opportunity. And as Jeff Bezos says, many are making decent money.

There are so many ways to supplement your income with a bit of extra cash, such as doing some extra hours in your week or get a second job, selling Tupperware or driving Uber. Amazon is a different opportunity. Amazon is your opportunity to build a pipeline business. It is a different model where you are not exchanging your time for cash, but instead gives you a ticket to escape the "hours for dollars" trap.

WHO CAN SUCCEED AT AMAZON?

So, who has this book been written for?

This book has been written for people who want to live life on their terms, and who want more control about how you spend their days.

Whether it's traveling more or living in a nicer home, getting rid of the mortgage…. these aspirational "dreams" can happen when you start to earn some extra income. These are some of the tangible benefits of an extra income.

This book also appeals to those wanting to live and work on their own terms, actively choosing how to spend their time, and with whom. The rat race is super tough: living and working in some of the worlds' largest cities is tough. Commuting is time consuming and that time is wasted. Think about how many hours in the week are wasted in long traffic congested journeys just getting to and from work each week.

Add to wasted time commuting the limited number of weeks holiday you're allocated with someone else dictating exactly when you take your time off. And then there's the office politics, the thankless bosses…… I could go on…..I will….
….There's always a crazy colleague or two, or a nightmare client or there's just all that energy and stress that goes into

surviving at work, never mind excelling at work.

Full-time work hours can be really demanding and take a real toll on our physical and mental health. And we're conditioned to accept that this is what we should do because it's what everyone elsedoes.

But maybe you're reading this book because you are hoping that there's a way out of the rat race I describe above. Maybe you're ready for a new challenge and a new way of doing things.

Maybe though, you're quite happy in your 9-5 corporate office job and the appeal of this book is to find a way to save for some big trips, or going to visit family on the other side of the world. Everyone will have their own personal reasons for wanting that extra income.

This book was written for people who want to do things a bit differently, take control of their personal circumstances and be rewarded with a sustainable source of extra income. This book was written for people like you who want to understand and learn about another way to earn extra income.

AMAZON: here's what I love about selling products on Amazon

Each and every day on Amazon there are millions of real people searching and shopping for items that they need. They may be consumer goods, food and grocery items, large items, small items, gifts and household supplies. With increasing demand for all kinds of products on Amazon, as sellers on the platform, our job is to sell them the things that they're looking for.

Some of the things that sell well are quite unglamorous. But there is always strong demand for these products and they always sell very well. An example of this type of product would be incontinence products or baby products. And, generally they are low cost recession-proof products.

I love the way that Amazon provides a service to customers who might otherwise not be able to get to the mall, or to the shops. Just think about the kinds of customers for whom going out to the shops is a bit of a hassle: the elderly, new moms, people stuck at the office.

I also love how Amazon appeals to my entrepreneurial side. I've always had an entrepreneurial itch and I was always going to start a business at some stage. Amazon came along at exactly the right time for me and I was able to take advantage of all the opportunities it presented.

Amazon also appealed to me because it's easy to set up and manage. The overheads are low (hey, I work from my kitchen table) and the set up swift. This meant that I could establish my business and get selling swiftly: I didn't need to spend my valuable time hiring staff, getting offices and all the other things that you usually have to do for business set up.

For me, and people in a similar position to me when starting out, I really believe that this is one of the best business models out there. Naturally, I might be a bit biased in singing the praises of an Amazon business, but I've walked the walk. I've been in the situation that you might find yourself in: a high demanding job, little time, limited control of that time etc.

Maybe you recognize some of these themes in your own personal situation, and if you do, I hope to share my journey with you and help you assess whether a professional Amazon pipeline business is the right venture for you.

"Use Amazon to beat the daily commute."

Great, sounds good - How soon can I quit my job?

Of course, learning the basics and learning how to establish a firm foundation for your Amazon business is critical and some investment of your time is essential. This is not a get rich quick scheme, and anyone who expects a million dollars to land into their bank account overnight will be disappointed.

To set things up thoroughly and start selling on Amazon takes a few months. In fact I decided to my day job for about nine months until I was really confident that the business was solid enough that I could quit my day job.

This is another benefit of starting an Amazon business; you don't have to quit your day job to start and grow it if you choose not to. You don't have to quit the day job to get the business up and running straight away. In fact, you can get things up and running without having to change any other commitment.

I made fifty-four thousand U.S. dollars of sales in an hour, whilst I was at the beach with the kids. Sure, that doesn't happen every day, but when it does happen, I can tell you that it feels super cool. All that was thanks to being able to partner with Amazon to establish my business relatively easily

Dear Boss,

I Quit

Love,
Sophie

The First Product in My Empire!

My first product actually cost about three hundred dollars to buy, I got seventy-five units and it was from Nepal.

That product turned into a million-dollar payday about a year later. Cash!

That was pretty exciting! I certainly didn't need to invest huge amounts of start-up capital in that product launch on Amazon.

The key to my first product was low capital investment and low risk. In fact, I get really annoyed when I see people out there talking about Amazon and telling people to go off and fill whole containers, because I like to de-risk the entire process as much as possible.

I blame my Scottish heritage; I'm very cautious. I never want to waste my money buying products that might not sell. Worse, I might get stuck with something I cannot sell. From my very first product launch on Amazon, I have always recommended that the market be tested with really small product quantities, with low risk.

If, then, that product doesn't sell for some reason, I don't have thousands of dollars (or thousands of pounds) at stake! Worst-case scenario, if I can't sell it, I drop the price until it does, and I've always been able to get my money back doing that.

De-risking is key to making your empire work!

But, if it is a good product and it's selling well, as it should, as your research has shown it should, then you can start ordering bigger shipments after that.

My approach is pretty conservative. I hate spending money and investing in products without making profit. In fact, there are many people making sales, but they don't actually bring any profit home. This is because they're trying to sell something that's too competitive or they've selected the wrong kind of products to sell on Amazon from the start.

So why listen to me?

You should listen and learn from me because I started my Amazon journey exactly where you'll be starting you own Amazon journey. I've walked the walk and made the mistakes so you don't have to. I will share my top tips and things to avoid, all based on my own personal experience. I'll guide you along the journey, starting at the beginning....

My first product cost me three hundred dollars to get going. Within fourteen months, that same product was generating $1.6 million US in sales, and then when I had been selling that product for about eighteen months old, I sold the account for over a million USD.

AMAZON BOOM 2020

Once I had enjoyed a healthy income from selling that product on Amazon, I approached a US investor to see if I could sell the business. I offered the business for sale for a cool million dollars and said, "if you want this business, I'll give you the Amazon password and you give me a million dollars". And that is exactly what we did.

That was my first business sale. Motivated and with a new set of skills I then started a second business. My second business was a tea business. I followed the same process of building the business as I had with my first business, and subsequently sold the second business for a few hundred thousand US dollars.

Prior to that point in my journey, my husband and I had both been working for the New Zealand government. I was working part-time to pay a nanny to look after the kids, so the numbers weren't great in the day job once my costs of working were paid. I certainly wasn't putting anything into a savings account let alone getting ahead financially.*

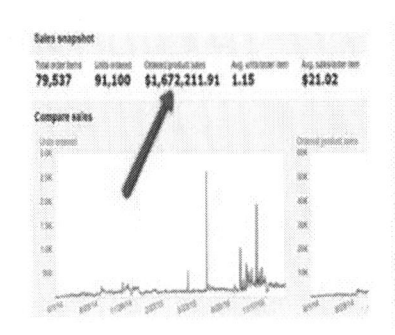

But—thanks to the Amazon business, the extra income it provided along the way and the cash received after not one, but two business sales, I was able to make some huge lifestyle changes.

---

*   Results not typical

The photo above is a place called Wanaka.

We chose to leave the big city, the day job and the daily grind and we chose to relocate to this idyllic town on the south end of New Zealand, where the kids get to go skiing on a Thursday with school. It's just amazing, and sometimes I have to pinch myself to check that I'm not dreaming—we're right up in the mountains and it's gorgeous. We have a great lifestyle and live really, really well.

Oh, also, before settling in Wanaka, we lived in Bali for three months after I sold the first business. This gave us, as a family, the opportunity to reconnect with each other and experience living in a different culture.

Naturally, people wanted to know the secret to my success. What I am doing on Amazon? How do I choose these products?

This is what I will be sharing with you in this book.

BUILDING YOUR EMPIRE FROM THE PRODUCTS FIRST!

Having sold about 500 different products on Amazon since starting my journey, I have worked out what kinds of products to source. I know the features and the characteristics of what makes for a profitable product; if the product is bulky and expensive, or prone to faults, or attracts customer complaints, then that's probably a product to avoid. Selecting the right kind of product to sell on Amazon is the most important consideration.

Then there's working with the suppliers. I've spent a lot of time working with suppliers all around the world. Some have been from China. My first suppliers were in Nepal.

I have also done a lot of successful sourcing in India, Bali and Sri Lanka. Some of my best productshave been sourced straight from the United States, especially for health products. Sourcing products in the US might be slightly higher than other regions of the world, but I don't like to have to undertake complicated overseas compliance paper-work to sell in the States.

So, I have a broad and thorough set of criteria that I look for in any product all captured in a checklist that I work through to identify the perfect product to sell on Amazon.

My extensive research into each and every product will take into consideration whether there's enough demand, enough people searching for that product. I also want to assess the profitability of each product I sell, and I want to make sure that there's not too much competition from other sellers.

Working with the right suppliers is not also an important consideration, it is critical to your business success! It's about knowing where to look for the right supplier, the questions to ask them. Once the right supplier has been found it's all about building a mutually beneficial business relationship. The importance of a supplier who is going to be reliable in producing consistent and high quality products cannot be underestimated. Choosing the right supplier is all about partnering and building a long-term business relationship, not simply a transactional relationship.

I put a lot of effort and energy into establishing and building strong partnerships with my suppliers. I see many people dealing with the same suppliers as me, and I hear how other Amazon sellers go about negotiating. Their focus is often all about the price: they're really focused on just getting the lowest price per unit and that can be a very short- term way to approach to building a profitable business.

I need my suppliers for the long term. Getting the lowest cost per unit is not my focus. I form really strong long-term relationships with them and ensure that I am building a mutually beneficial relationship with my suppliers from the start.

Building strong relationships with my suppliers has also led to some amazing and unique experiences for me: I have been invited to weddings - one in Nepal, one in China - it's a real partnership!

I get a lot of other benefits from building strong relationships with my suppliers: they give me the "inside scoop" on where I should invest my time and my money. They feed me great product ideas. They tell me what my competitors are up to.

They really help me grow my business.

A good relationship with a supplier can really be a kind of secret weapon in getting ahead. Finding the right products and working with great suppliers is one of the most important elements of my business.

Once you have identified the right products and found the right suppliers, you will want to accelerate and grow your business and you will want to put systems in place to make the business run smoothly and makes life easy for you. This is especially important if you still have your day job. One of the best ways make your business efficient and to make sure that your time and resources are not over stretched is to make Amazon do all the heavy lifting. This is another reason that I love Amazon businesses so much. Amazon does all the hard work and all the heavy lifting.

Of course, there are many different ways to sell on Amazon; some ways are more profitable than others, some ways are harder work than others. The best way to sell on Amazon ensures that you are profitable where low- touch methods are used. These are my preferred methods to use when selling on Amazon. We're going to cover this more in depth later in the book.

Having sold a couple of Amazon businesses, I now know that there are a few things that need to be done at the start that ensures that my business looks really attractive when it's put on the market and listed for sale. I didn't know these when I first started out on Amazon, but I know them now and I'll share these with you.

If you've sold a business before, you know it's a big transaction. It's not the sort of thing you do too many times in a lifetime, so it's important to get it right when the (few) opportunities do arise to sell a successful business.

If, from the moment you establish your business, you can make a few changes that enables a potential buyer to purchase your business swiftly, or better, to buy your business in cash, with no "earn out" period, you'll be delighted that you were following this system when you started things up.

WHAT IS AMAZON TODAY AND HOW COULD IT MAKE ME CASHFLOW?

When Amazon first launched, it was an online bookstore. Amazon still sell lots of books and e-books, but they rapidly evolved and grew. Amazon is now The Everything Store. Everyone shops on Amazon. Perhaps you do a lot of your shopping on Amazon too.

What sets Amazon apart is its scale. Amazon sells billions of dollars worth of products per month. It's a staggeringly huge company. And within Amazon are customers who have developed loyalty to particular brands selling particular products.

Let's consider an example. If you are a serious golfer, the purchase of a golf club is very important: you will probably purchase a big brand name golf club partly for its high performance, but also because you identify with the brand behind the product. And someone who identifies with a brand is loyal to that brand, and if a person is loyal to the brand, they will purchase that brands products.

But let's consider other products. There are many products that get purchased where a customer does not identify with the brand (if that product even has a brand). Products like this might include bookends or mirrors or candle holders.

The buyer doesn't really care what the brand is, it just has to look the part, be good quality and be exactly what it looks like in the photo (if being purchased online).

Amazon recognized this very quickly. So much so, that they actually launched thousands of Amazon Home Brand products. As an extension of their own Home Brand product ranges, Amazon has now started letting other people to sell on its extensive platform.

The products that other sellers offer on the Amazon platform don't really have any big loyalty to the brand name, and these products are the perfect ones to sell on Amazon.

These products are often simple products with relatively low price tags; the sweet spot being $20-$30USD.

If a product is really, really cheap it's hard to make any profit. At the other end of the spectrum, if a product is really expensive people want to see it in person. If it's something that's really high performance or have technical electronic capabilities, these are quite hard to sell on Amazon, as the buyer will want to test or experience an expert demonstration prior to purchase.

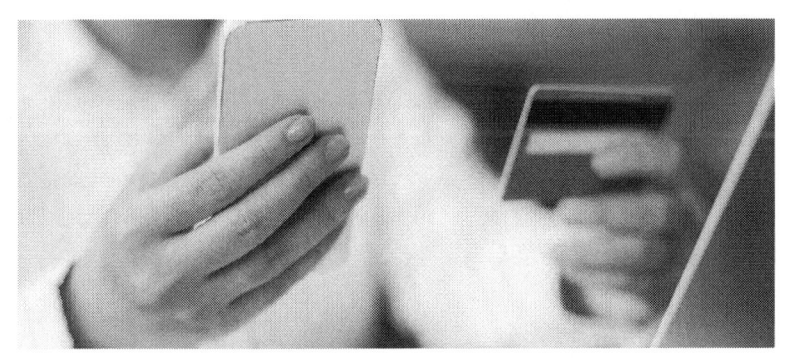

All other products have the potential to sell well on Amazon. Everything else goes! Beauty products, health products, sports gear, baby gear, toys - you name it, Amazon probably sells it.

Food and grocery products also have the potential to sell well on Amazon. My last business was a tea business. Selling food with a shelf life, or perishable products, is possible but they can be quite tricky. I prefer products that are "low drama", the types of products that you can just forget, whilst you spend time developing your next product launch. That's my favorite kind of business.

Anything goes on Amazon and I have a lot of fun, researching, digging and scampering around looking for little pockets where not everybody else is selling.

In the United States, there have been people selling Amazon pretty seriously for a while now. As a result, some of the really obvious products have too many sellers with similar or identical products. This over competitive situation ends up in ugly price wars. The seller willing to take the lowest price gets the sale. I never want to sell a product where the competitive advantage is price alone.

Again, let's look at an example: Yoga mats, gym supplements or protein powders attract many sellers. It becomes too hard to make money on these types of products because there are simply too many sellers selling similar products to each other.

I much prefer to duck and dive around, stay under the radar and have a portfolio of products that have much lower risk, with higher profits and limited competition. I really focus on low competition products.

A LITTLE BIT ABOUT JEFF AND HOW HE MAKES ME SERIOUS MONEY

Jeff Bezos founded Amazon 22 years ago. He used to be a hedge fund trader. He's a pretty smart guy. He is really aggressive. He does not like to lose.

He now has so much money behind him as the world's richest man; he just over took Warren Buffet.

He's also known for being quite experimental, pushing boundaries and trying new things. One of his latest projects is a patented a system to stop drone deliveries of his products being shot down by bow and arrow! Bezos is taking Amazon, and the world on e-Commerce and online shopping to new places. He's developing floating warehouses. In his spare time, he does space exploration using his own money!

So, Bezos is wealthy and aggressive. He's wildly competitive and generally does not play nicely with others. If a company is in his way and he wants to get into that sector, or expand into a new geographical territory, he'll persist with his plan, undermine the competition so that they eventually fragment. He'll then gobble up that competitor by buying them out. This puts him in a position where he can dominate either sectors, or sometimes even entire geographical regions.

Compared to the now Jeff Bezos of the 90's he's even looking tough and mean lately, seriously pumping iron and wearing dark sunglasses! Behind that cool facade, he's putting huge effort into his businesses and he is not slowing down at all.

SOPHIE HOWARD

1998: "I sell books." *2017: "I sell whatever the F*** I want."*

Jeff Bezos's business plan for Amazon was extremely aggressive: He made all the investors who backed Amazon 20 years ago wait for 10 years to see any profit because he was reinvesting that profit and buying up big warehouses, shipping lines and start-ups. He was building delivery fleets and exploring expansion opportunities into new countries and new regions of the world. With such dominance, he's untouchable.

Bezos recently spent three billion dollars establishing Amazon in India. They just opened Amazon Australia which has big opportunities for sellers: all the American sellers will completely ignore the Australian market, so we are going to have a lot of fun cleaning up all the sales down here.

Amazon is a truly global business. With Amazon infrastructure extending to so many countries around the world, as a seller on Amazon you can be based anywhere in the world and sell anywhere that Amazon operates. As a seller with an Amazon business, so many markets are open to you.

Most Amazon sellers start in the States, expanding then to the UK and Europe. Then they start selling on Amazon in Australia. Finally, a seller might expand into the Indian market. Keep up to date with Amazon's expansion plans to discover new unique opportunities: The next Amazon market to open will be South Korea.

Amazon recently bought a huge website in the Middle East called Souq.com, and so the middle East will soon present sellers with new market opportunities.

How to take advantage of the golden Amazon opportunity

If the Amazon opportunity is one too good to pass for you, let's talk nuts and bolts:

Let's talk about what you need to get set up as a seller on Amazon.

First of all, understand that you can be based anywhere in the world to sell on Amazon. I live in New Zealand and sell on Amazon in the United States. It cost

$50USD a month to have an Amazon account. On that account, you can have as many brands and as many products as you wish.

Amazon doesn't impose quota's on the number of products you have listed, or on the quantity of each product to be sold. It's up to you entirely. What you charge for a product is your choice. You have complete control.

In addition to being able to control your price and the amount inventory held, you can choose to trade as just an individual on Amazon. This means that you can get started quickly as you don't have to start a company. However, many sellers choose to set up as a business from the start. The income generated from your Amazon sales is treated as any other income and will be subject to taxes in your home country.

This is something to chat to your accountant about, as he/she will be able to advise you based on your own personal circumstances.

If you want to take advantage of the US Amazon market place, there is no need to visit the USA or set up a company and bank accounts in the USA.

Payments based on the sales made are paid back to you regularly. Amazon pays out every two weeks and will deposit monies back to your own bank account, wherever that may be.

This whole process is undertaken online, so you can be a "digital and do" business completely.

Imagine…. you could be on the beach in Bali or in Australia or in the UK, wherever, it doesn't matter, you just need to list your products where the customers are. After that you can simply keep expanding around the world with Amazon, so your company becomes global swiftly and with ease.

Last year more than 55% of all product searches in the US started on Amazon.

Wow. What does that mean?

It means that people don't turn to Google to go shopping. They actually go to Amazon. In fact Amazon is such a trusted market place that a quarter of people about to purchase a product in a retail store will look that product up on Amazon for reviews and feedback about that product.

I am sure that the product being researched is actually cheaper on Amazon! Add to this free shipping offered to many Amazon customers, it's no surprise that Amazon is fast becoming the preferred shopping method for millions and millions of people.

Once a year, Amazon does a huge promotion to get customers to sign up to their shipping membership program. On that day, while they are promoting a wide range of products, Amazon can process 600 items per second coming off the conveyor belts; products being picked up by robots off the shelves, getting labeled with the customer's address and given to a delivery driver. All those purchased products make it to the doorsteps of those customers. Amazon is an incredible machine with unbelievable scale.

Amazon's shipping capability and infrastructure is enormous, so much so that it is now competing with UPS, FedEx and other companies that offer standalone shipping services.

Amazon purchases amount to $136 billion a year, which equates to $380 million dollars a day. The value of the company has now surpassed $1 trillion.

As I said, Jeff Bezos is very aggressive commercially. His plan is to be the first trillion- dollar company. One of the ways that he is expanding Amazon is by letting more people like us sell more of our products on the Amazon platform.

In order to take advantage of selling on the Amazon platform, we don't need to invent or design a product. We simply have to go through a process of registering as a seller and listing our products. We simply need to undertake some research to identify what's in demand and what product categories are not too competitive. Then we need to start selling those products ourselves. Amazon makes it simple to sell online. They do all the heavy lifting.

I love this analogy: There's a huge river of cash and products changing hands every day, people spending money on Amazon with their credit cards loaded. As a seller, you just need to tap into that flow and have some of that money surfacing back to you via your bank account.

Until recently, most products sold "on" Amazon were sold "by" Amazon. But this has changed and now more than half of all units purchased on Amazon are sold by 3rd party sellers, and these sellers are often regular people like you and me: People with day jobs, people from different countries in the world are selling products on Amazon in their spare time to generate some extra cash.

Jeff Bezos, in being so commercially competitive and aggressive, has created the perfect platform for us, private 3rd party sellers, to build lucrative businesses. Bezos has made it so easy for us to build our businesses on his platform.

Here is what a private 3rd party successful business on Amazon looks like: One of my Amazon accounts generates over $2.3 million USD in sales from the sale of 131,000 units ordered online. Amazingly, of the 131,000 units sold, I didn't physically touch a singleone.*

---

*   Results not typical

Date	Sales breakdown	Product category	Fulfillment channel
Custom 01/09/2015 – 01/09/2017	Marketplace total	All product categories	Both (Amazon and seller)

Sales snapshot taken at January 9, 2017 at 5:42 PM PST

Total order items	Units ordered	Ordered product sales	Avg. units/order item	Avg. sales/order item
115,794	131,404	$2,337,602.99	1.13	$20.19

That's right, **I did not put my hands on a single one** of those products. **Amazon did everything for me** to make those sales. I love a business where I can be completely hands-off and yet I still achieve those sales numbers.

So, does Amazon sound like quite an interesting company to you, and one you may want to partner with?

"They do the hard work, so you don't need to!"

SOPHIE HOWARD

HOW TO PUT YOUR AMAZON BUSINESS ON AUTOPILOT

How does Amazon manage to sell up to 600 units per second? and how is it I manage to have a day where I sold $54,000 in sales while I was at the beach?

Well, Amazon offers a unique service called, "Fulfilled by Amazon", also known as FBA and it's a partnership; you list products for sale on the Amazon platform, and Amazon deals with all the customer service. This is Amazon's point of difference: they really want to control the customer experience.

So much so that Amazon is now one of the top brands for customer service. In fact, Amazon is the #1 most trusted brand in the United States because the customer service is second to none. Amazon's delivery to door service is super smooth, and goods arrive as they should and in perfect condition. Amazon has really perfected this whilst many other companies suffer from providing poor customer service with tracking numbers, delivery delays and sometimes even goods not being delivered.

Quite simply, people love shopping on Amazon and Amazon really loves giving those customers superior service and smooth "one-click" order experiences. That's why Amazon has been so successful; they are obsessed with the customer experience.

So, if you choose to become a 3rd party private seller on Amazon, how does it work? Well, in a nutshell, Amazon keeps all of your products in their warehouses, and when orders are received for those products, Amazon will deliver them to customers on your behalf – all for a flat fee of around $50 per month plus a small fee for each product sold.

And this unique FBA service allows you to make great money, even while you're at the beach!

One day whilst I was at the beach with my kids, I was checking the little app on my phone that keeps an eye on my sales. I was tracking it throughout the day. Just after our lunch picnic at the beach, I hit refresh on the app and was astounded to see that my sales had not only spiked, they had gone through the roof! I'd done

$54,000USD in sales in one hour. Amazon was seeing my product in stock. Amazon also saw that customers really liked my product and so they decided that they are going to do a promotion, which generated enormous sales. All this whilst I was building sand castles at the beach with my kids!

Amazon didn't tell me they were going to do a promotion. They just did it. My sales just went through the roof thanks to that Amazon promotion. I was still in control of my price and all those products sold at full price. The fees charged by Amazon are based on my sale price. Usually about 1/3 of the selling price goes to Amazon, about 1/3 goes to you as profit and about 1/3 is due to the cost of buying and shipping in the United States.

So, let's walk through a quick calculation:

From my $54,000.00USD* sales hour, around $18,000 was mine to keep. That's an incredible number. How many hours, days, weeks or months would it take to earn that in a day job? And you definitely couldn't be at the beach making sand castles while you make that kind of money.

---

*   Results not typical

But, strangely, it wasn't quite as exciting as my very first sale. The first sale you get is like a "miracle ofAmazon".

At first it can feel quite surreal. You've done some product research. You send some money overseas to purchase a product (that you're going to sell on Amazon) to someone you've never met via an international bank transfer. Then you get that product shipped with all the right labels. It goes right through the ports, through customs and arrives at an Amazon warehouse on the other side of the world.

Then that product shows up for sale on the Amazon platform. A customer comes along and searches for it on Amazon, orders it over the competition and pays Amazon. Miraculously, you see your bank balance on Amazon go from zero to $20!

It's amazing, that 1st sale is more exciting than these really big numbers you get later down the track.

I had another amazing sales day before I'd resigned from my day job. I had a $33,000 sales day and I remember just sitting at my work desk in my office and wondering why I was even at work! (Results not typical).

These sales numbers are possible once you have the right product and play by Amazon's rules. The opportunity to sell products on Amazon and make serious income is very real.

"I sold $54,000 of products in 1 hour- while at the beach...."*

Every day, there are new products that Amazon customers are searching for. There are 150 million Amazon customers in the United States. Nine million of them are millionaires so there is a real opportunity to use the Amazon platform to sell high value, high quality products.

Amazon is not a just a budget platform at all.

Beyond the US market are other significant market opportunities. There are 300 million+ potential customers in Europe, over 100 million customers in the States, millions more in India, and it all is still growing. Using the Amazon sales platform as 3rd party sellers, we can start completely global from day one. That represents an enormous opportunity.

If you were starting out with a regular products business the cost of set up and growth would be significant: you would be looking at cementing a national company and you would be hiring a Lawyer and a Tax Advisor and getting all the paperwork in order.

Once the business was established, you would need some

---

*   Results not typical

people on the ground getting commissions and salaries. You would need vehicles, a warehouse, inventory and a courier company. You'd also need customer service team for invoicing and returns and maybe a marketing team. It's a real expense to start a company, but not so with an Amazon business.

If you choose to set yourself up as a 3rd party Amazon seller…..

… Amazon handles all of that so you don't have to!

Think of the money saved before you even start selling on Amazon.

You don't need to do any external marketing to raise awareness about your product because customers are already on Amazon searching and shopping. Quite simply, you just need to sell the products that they are looking for. Customers on Amazon are ready to shop. Their credit cards are loaded and they're searching for products to BUY. So, if you're selling products that customers are searching for and your product images are accurate, you're good to go. People are shopping online more and more (it's a terrible time to be in conventional or offline retail)

Think of the lifestyle you can build around this kind of business. You can be anywhere in the world. You just need Wi-Fi. How good is that?

As a 3rd party Amazon seller, you don't need to build your own website or run Facebook ads. You don't need to do customer service. You don't need to build your own brand because people trust Amazon. You don't need to lease an office, you don't need to hire employees, you don't need to work huge hours, you don't need to spend thousands of dollars to choose and develop products. And, you don't need to be very "techy' to do this at all.

You have the potential to earn in this business what you used to earn in your day job but in a fraction of the time.

You don't need to work 24/7. You don't need a desk and there are no HR requirements, no meaningless meetings, no lengthy conference calls.

As well as selling products on Amazon as a 3rd party seller, there are also other opportunities for income generation using Amazon.

One of the things I did before I left my day job was to review 4 companies whose products are used in homes but weren't on Amazon.

I actually approached these companies to see if they had the appetite for selling on Amazon. My question to those companies went something like this: "do you want me to set up and run your Amazon business?" All said "yes please" and I quickly replaced my day job salary with just 4 of those 'accounts'. This is just another way you can profit from Amazon.

Having achieved some success by selling great products on Amazon, I am on a real mission to share my knowledge and everyday people find the right kind of products to sell on Amazon.

Amazon is attracting a very diverse range of 3rd party sellers. People are really coming into Amazon and starting sell from all sorts of different backgrounds. For example, one of my students is a fireman, another runs a laundromat business in Sydney and another works in a bank.

Third party Amazon sellers are drawn from different walks of life, and many of them have no particular "techy" background. Even if you don't consider yourself "techy" you can still sell on Amazon. What actually makes a successful seller is actually how good you are at choosing the right kind of products to sell on Amazon.

In this book, I'm going to share with you all I have learned about choosing the right kind of products to sell on Amazon.

HOW TO FIND WINNING PRODUCTS TO SELL ON AMAZON

Let's have a look at what these "good" products may look like.

1. **First, I like products that have a 30% profit margin.**

2. **Secondly, I like repeat purchase products.** It's much easier to sell to an existing satisfied customer than it is to sell a one-off high-priced item such as an electronic product or other products that have a high price tag. Customers prefer to buy products with a high price tag in person.

Most third party Amazon sellers choose a product that is already selling with a really high volume of sales. Then they copy that product, reverse engineer it and do a "knock off". Sellers following this model will find a supplier, cut down the price, make some tiny tweaks and then hope to get a chunk of the market share.

But I don't like that model, partly because of the ethics and partly because if you can do that to someone else what's stopping them from doing it to you.

The other reason I avoid this model (and its actually what most of the other mainstream Amazon educators teach) where I am forced to chase the best selling products because this model requires a massive upfront investment to compete. And because your product is not differentiated, you very quickly end up in a price war. It's a model I don't like at all.

Now, I like to operate differently. I have a system of selecting products so I don't need to reinvent the wheel again each time I go to choose a new one. I know what makes a good Amazon product and that's what I look for. I am very focused on the type of product I am looking for. I am also very focused on what products to avoid.

This methodology and the way I choose products means I have never been copied or had to compete on price.

Let me share with you an example of how I select the best products to sell on Amazon.

One of my products sells for $28 for a pack of 4. The next best product was a bigger pack size and sold for $9.99 – How is that possible? It all comes down to choosing a good product and one where you can get onto the first page of search results for a keyword that enough customers are searching for.

80% of Amazon success is in product selection and having a smart strategy to choose low competition winners. Product selection is critical to your success on Amazon.

Once you have identified a product with low competition, it's to build a great Amazon "listing" for that product so that you can showcase that product to potential customers searching on Amazon.

To do that you will need to get professional photographs of your product taken. You will also need to write a description for your product that tells customers exactly what theproductdoes. Writing a listing is easy when you know how. Whilst product imagery and product descriptions are important, the game is won and lost in the product selection. I see so many people make terrible choices because they don't know what they're looking for or what to avoid.

"The secret is...PRIVATE LABELLING - with a twist."

So, what I like to do is give a "facelift" to a basic product. Even if it might be a basic commodity product like tea, there is always part of the market where people will pay premium pricing for organic tea or tea from certified heavy metal free soil. Perhaps its being packaged differently to ensure freshness, or the pickers and tea growers get a levy from me and my payments go towards education of their family.

Millennial customers (all of whom shop on Amazon) really care about the story behind the product or how the purchase of the product is improving the lives of the people who make it.

Sometimes, the way to set a product apart from the competition is simply better design, or better packaging. Products where the design and packaging are custom designed and really stand out can command a premium price, especially if it's a gifting type of product.

There are other things that you can do to a product to give it a facelift. Maybe you can offer a free gift or add an information product.

Let'sl ook at a good example; say they buy coconut oil. The product could be a jar of coconut oil, or soap, or pet shampoo. You can work directly with the manufacturer and come up with your own label for that product.

You don't need to be a designer to do this. Instead you hire a designer.

I usually find a designer online and I pay them anything from $20 - $50. If you are going to be working with a designer, its critical that you provide a thorough brief. And to provide a good brief, you need to have first undertaken some research on Amazon.

You would work with your designer having researched what's selling well on Amazon. You will have a good understanding of demographic that buys this product, and you would brief your designer accordingly. You may have some minor compliance tests to undertake but you can work with the manufacturer on this.

Essentially though, it may just be packaging the product and making it "look the part". This may be all that's needed to ensure that customers are willing to pay premium price for this particular product.

The text on your labels and the look and feel of the packaging is important.

More than the physical features of the product, the labeling and packaging needs to convey the benefits of the product, or an element of the product that makes it truly unique or special. Is it organic? Is it fair trade? Is it sourced from pristine tropical-island in the pacific? Does it support charity?

Alternatively, can you add something to the product that enhances the value of the product? Can you offer a free recipe book? Can you create a video showing ten different skincare applications for coconut oil?

I always try to add value to my products. These "extras" can cost very little, and some may be free, but they can give your product a real point of difference. This also makes it really hard for competitors to copy. In fact, I've never had anyone copy one of my five hundred Amazon products, which is pretty unusual.

The main reason my products work is that customers are surprised and delighted by the extra effort taken to make your product stand out. It might be that the packaging is thoughtfully considered, or perhaps it's the story behind the product. Alternatively, it could simply be the quality of the product or the fact that it's from a unique source. I have so much fun with this.

I find inspiration for unique points of difference for products from many places. Sometimes I get inspiration from online sources. But sometimes, I go to see what's happening on the pharmacy retail shelves for a product similar to the one I'm about to launch. I like to see how different products look and how they feel. I like to see what's working for other products to enable me to enhance my own online sales.

As long as your brief to your designer is clear and well thought out, the private label designer can be from anywhere in the world.

In the past I have worked with some world-class Colombian designers. I also work with designers closer to home and have a few that I love working with who are based in New Zealand.

When selecting a designer to work with, its important to look at their portfolio of past work. If searching for a freelance designer from an online source (Fiverr. com for example) I like to do some investigating by reading through the reviews of other people who have worked with them.

Once you have provided your designer with a clear brief based on your research of the market on Amazon, it's then time to turn your attention to thinking about Amazon customers, and specifically, how exactly they shop on Amazon.

If you shop for products online, think about how you shop. Also think about what devices you are using to shop online: a lot of people are going to be scrolling on their phones to shop. If they are shopping on their smartphones to shop, it is likely that they're not going to have any attention span for lengthy product descriptions. As such it's important to stand out visually. You have to convey the look and feel of your product clearly. Your product must jump off the page and leave all the competition else behind.

This strategy for selling products on Amazon is private labeling, but it is more than just private labeling. It is private labeling with a twist.

So let's have a look at some examples. Let's consider coffee. Of course, there are people who are happy to have instant coffee. On the other end of the spectrum there are people who are really quite serious about their coffee, so much so that they will happily pay a lot more for the gourmet version, or the freshest beans, or the strongest coffee, or whatever it may be. You get the idea.

We'll look at some other examples later in the book that demonstrate that every product exists within a range of products. How third-party sellers make their money is by taking a basic product but dressing it up with great packaging, a great story and a good point of difference.

I have first hand experience of taking a basic product, but doing it well (and making a lot of money in the process). My tea brand is a perfect example. Tea is a commodity product that's been traded for centuries. But nobody on Amazon had done an organic loose leaf tea in beautiful packaging that was really freshly packed. I took the basic product and I made it better. I also had a really good story to tell about how I worked with the supply chain, sourcing from exotic places and supporting local communities.

I positioned the product well, so it meant I could buy it for a dollar and sell it for $22. That's an amazing mark up. Also, for customers, it was a repeat purchase, so the business model was great. It was such an attractive profitable business that I actually ended up selling that tea business to another bigger tea business.

I sold my first business to an investor who simply wanted the cash flow. The second business I sold was to an Indian family business that sells tea, but they just didn't have an online business. They were happy to pay a significant sum of cash for an already built, plug and play online Amazon business.

These types of Amazon businesses have a real value. I didn't intend to sell my first business, but I asked an online business broker for some advice about what the business was worth when it was about eighteen months old. The value of the business was about $1 million USD, but that's only interesting if someone is actually willing and able to pay that amount of money for that kind of business. Because my little Amazon business was set up correctly, it was very attractive to a range of investors. That same broker suggested listing the business for sale, and a buyer came forward to purchase my business.

It goes without saying that those lump sums are real game changers; they enable you to pay off a mortgage, or make some investments. Quite suddenly life changes dramatically.

SOPHIE HOWARD

So here's a real example of an Amazon product.

This is a product selling on Amazon in the United States. It sells for $12.97 USD.*

It is a pack of four toothbrushes that have some fancy bristles. They're presented in a nice box and they have private labeled packaging.

A minimal amount of effort has been put in to making the product stand out. The seller has probably spent a total of $20 on getting some nice packaging designed and a logo created.

The fee owed to Amazon for selling that product is $1.95. The F.B.A fee (that's the fulfillment fee for Amazon to ship the product out to the customer) is $2.43. The cost of the toothbrushes themselves plus the shipping into Amazon would probably cost about $2.50.

That's a total cost of $6.88, which leaves a profit of $6.09 per unit. So, this seller is making about $6.09 profit per unit.

This product is selling approximately 1060 units per month

---

* Rough example for illustrative purposes only and is based on estimated numbers. Do you own due diligence on any potential product before selling it.

which equates to $6400 USD per month estimated PROFIT from just one product.

Before you rush out and decide to sell bamboo toothbrushes, let me tell you that this actually wouldn't be a great product to do simply because it was so easy to find their supplier. This would actually be a product that is too easy to copy.

However, I wanted to illustrate how easy it can be to get going. If you consider the start- up costs here, it is minimal. An investment in this kind of product would probably cost 0.30 to 0.50 per piece and you only need to buy 300 of them to get states.

HOW TO FIND THE HOTTEST PRODUCTS

Toothbrushes – Selling for	$12.97 USD
Less Amazon fees	-$1.95
Less FBA fees	-$2.43
Toothbrushes & shipping	-$2.50
	$6.09 profit per unit

1060 units per month… $6,455.50 USD or $8,407 AUD

Generally, I avoid products that are this cheap and this easy to source because the fact that they are cheap and easy to source means that the barrier to entry for this type of product is relatively low. Anyone can do it which means that the competition can come in very quickly. If you start selling well, other sellers have the opportunity to copy you easily. I prefer products that require a bit more work up front which make them more difficult to copy.

The advantage of a product that is cheap and easy to source is that the cost of launching these products on Amazon can be very low. My advice would be to look for a product that's a bit more expensive, and a little harder to source from a manufacturer. When you have a product that commands a higher price and is difficult to copy, the numbers get even better and you have the opportunity to make more profit.

Who would like a product like that to sell on Amazon?

F.B.A. fees that Amazon charge are for delivering the product to the customers. They only charge you that once you've made the sale.

You pay the $40 per month and then Amazon deducts some fees after you've made sales but not before you made sales so you're never of out of pocket with Amazon.

Amazon also handles all the returns. Part of choosing a good product is that there shouldn't be too many returns. It's a metric I keep an eye on but I don't worry about it as I don't need to do anything about it.

If it was creeping up I would have a look at what's going on, but it's usually like a fraction of a percent in any category. A category that gets lots of returns is usually clothing.

To make your business work, you really need to know all your numbers. I've got a big spreadsheet that makes sure when you're researching product, you really know those numbers.

The key point is though that you're only one step away from new levels of success and freedom on Amazon.

WHAT'S YOUR FIRST STEP TO BUILDING YOUR GLOBAL AMAZON EMPIRE?

If you're serious about breaking free from the constraints of a conventional job, actually taking control of your life and building a lifestyle of abundance that you deserve, you really need to take action right now.

Because if you don't, there's a high chance it'll never happen.

We all know what it's like to put something off for a day, which then becomes a week, which then becomes a month, then before you know it, a year has passed and you're still stuck in the same dead-end job making someone else rich.

But there's another problem – I see so many people making serious mistakes with their Amazon business that they lose tons of money up front, get demotivated and never manage to crack the code properly. They never get to realize their dream because they didn't start on the right track.

I don't want that to happen to you. I SERIOUSLY don't want you to fall into some of the same, easy-to-make mistakes I made. I want this to be easy for you.

Exercise 1:

What is your 'big' why for starting an Amazon business?
More time with family? Money for holidays?
Quit your current job? A secure retirement?
What are your three big motivators?

Understanding your why and revisiting it often will help you stay motivated. It will also shape the action you take now.

1. _____

2. _____

3. _____

CHAPTER TWO

HOW AMAZON THINKS

In this chapter, I want to help you understand how Amazon thinks.

Amazon is an enormous, trillion-dollar business. Amazon is also the number one most trusted brand in the United States. They are doing something really special to be this big and with so few actual employees.

In general, there is no staff fronting Amazon to ensure the customer experience is a favorable one. Except for the delivery driver, it is purely an online experience for the customer.

Quite simply, Amazon has nailed the whole customer experience and has done a great job of gaining trust and confidence.

What has Amazon done to be so trustworthy? Why do customers shop on Amazon?

As professional sellers, when we partner with Amazon selling on that huge global platform, what are we doing for them and what are they doing for us?

Rather than this chapter talking about the nuts and bolts of how fulfillment by Amazon works, I will help you understand what drives Amazon as a business. How their "customer culture" is what they stand for, what they live for and what they are obsessed with.

In this short chapter I will explain why Amazon is obsessed with the customer experience. In fact, the number one driver for Amazon is not profit, volume, market share or how many countries in the world they operate in.

For Amazon, the number one measurement is whether the customer is happy. Amazon wants to ensure an outstanding experience for each and every customer. This is what drives Amazon.

Providing a great customer experience the most important part of their corporate culture all the way from the top of the organization, right to the bottom.

MEET JEFF

Jeff Bezos's pioneering entrepreneurial spirit and successful business ventures has made him one of the wealthiest men in the world.

He is the founder and CEO of Amazon. His first job after graduation was as a Wall Street trader, becoming the youngest senior vice president.

Four years later he resigned and started the Amazon.com journey. He is intelligent and the way he goes about business will give insight into what you need to know about Amazon.

An example I'll share with you is the first domain name he registered when he started his business: It was relentless.com. You can look at any web hosting site now to see if you can buy relentless.com, you will see that Jeff Bezos owns that one.

"Relentless" is wired into his brain. That's his mentality. He is like a bulldozer. He plays a long game and is not flashy with his marketing. He doesn't promise people a quick win.

He wants to make sure that the customer has a great experience and that he builds a solid business that will keep growing, because if the customer is looked after and they have a great experience buying on Amazon, that customer will come back to purchase more products again and again and again.

THE EVERYTHING STORE

I recommend reading *"The Everything Store"*. This will give you more insights into

Jeff Bezos and an understanding of how Amazon works.

Amazon calls itself *"The Everything Store"* because it wants to sell all products to all people. For example, if nobody is selling diapers on Amazon, Jeff Bezos will go out and buy a company that sells diapers. He is able to quickly plug that gap and make sure his customers, who are buying diapers, have a great range of diapers.

The pricing has to be good, the range and choice has to be there and it has to be a quality product.

To improve on this even further, building on good pricing and good choice, Amazon ensures that once chosen the product is delivered to the customer swiftly. To ensure this, Amazon has a far reaching infrastructure of warehouses and delivery fleets.

They are obsessed with the customer experience.

When you read *"The Everything Store"*, you will understand how Amazon assesses new opportunities. You will understand how the company identifies new gaps in the market and establishes new efficient systems and process. Amazon famously patented the one-click payment option.

When you buy on Amazon you can now press the "buy now" button. In one click the product will be in your cart, charged to your credit card and shipped.

Your chosen product is on its way to you in one click.

PARTNER WITH #1

Amazon has revolutionized e-commerce, and it doesn't have any close competition.

Companies in the USA such as Walmart are trying to catch up by doing crazy things such as paying their staff to deliver parcels on their way home from work! None of Amazons competitors have the infrastructure to store millions of different products and get them delivered to the customer's doorstep swiftly. The logistics are horrendously complex.

Amazon has huge volumes of products going through its warehouses. Each warehouse, plus the delivery fleets, enables them to be efficient with their costing but also get real economy ofscale.

With this scale and efficiency, the customer wins everytime- with fast,cost effective, reliable ordering and delivery.

Amazon wants to sell everything, and it wants to cover all categories. In fact, when Amazon didn't have enough of the weekly household spend on grocery items, it actively went out and spent $13 billion buying Whole Foods Market.

This is another insight into Jeff Bezoz' relentless nature.

Similarly, when Amazon went into baby products, they actively bought startup companies and existing brands and launched them on Amazon. Quite simply, they bought the competitors that were in their way.

Amazon has very deep pockets and large budgets to work with when they want to make a strategic move.

No one is immune to failure and Amazon have had a couple of failures over the 20 something years. For example, the Amazon warehouse fire originated from one of their own products: an Amazon branded mobile phone.

However, very few Amazon projects fail. They are very ambitious, and they are happy to take risks. If an idea has a low probability of working, they are still happy to give it a go as they can financially support it. If it works, it will be huge. It might take 10 years of really intensive financing to get there, but they can do it, so they do.

They don't compete with projects that other people like Walmart or Costco can do themselves. They are more focused on the futuristic projects that have the potential to revolutionize whole sectors of the economy.

Amazon has even patented technologies such as systems to defend their drone deliveries from being shot down by bow and arrow!

Amazon has also researched floating warehouses that hover off the ground. The company has also investigated warehouses situated in ocean going ships, sitting just off the coast to help them get tax effectiveness.

AMAZON GETS THE EDGE

Amazon is smart; their teams work out what will give them an edge, what will make customers enjoy the experience even more and what will give them long term profitability.

They certainly don't worry about short-term profitability.

Jeff Bezos has an amazing ability to front a room full of analysts from Wall Street and announce, "We're launching in South Korea. We've bought souk.com, we've bought Whole Foods Market for $13 billion."

These are huge moves that are very bold. Jeff Bezos is a fantastic storyteller.

If any other company came out with some of the plans that Amazon announces, their share price would tumble and people would be spooked. It would not help the business because they sound so futuristic and too risky.

In contrast, when Amazon makes these announcements and Jeff Bezos unveils his vision for the business, he has absolute command and leadership, 23 years and counting.

When he makes announcements, he captivates hard, dry, analysts. He is able to level with some of the world's top analytical people because he is able to speak their language and present numbers, strategic plans and business plans in a compelling way.

Analysts love Bezos and his creativity. In fact, they seem to be very forgiving of his eccentricities, his ambitious schemes and projects that sound improbable. Bezos is a great storyteller and is able to explain his vision with clarity. His plans for the company sound futuristic, but he is able to build a compelling case. His plans make sense.

His audience can see the potential of his plans. He has built a strong track record of success that analysts and investors trust him to succeed with his ambitious projects. They don't associate Bezos with failure in any way.

I think Wall Street finds Jeff Bezos approach very refreshing.

In his days prior to Amazon, Bezos was an analyst on Wall Street He was a hedge fund manager. With experience in the finance and investment sector he knows how to announce his updates and explain his results. He understands how those people think. He knows what makes them tick.

Jeff Bezos manages his own reputation. He is a hard and ambitious businessman. He is driven and focuses on growth.

Because he tells a good story and is trusted, his investors have waited patiently so to see the big investment return that is now starting to flow from the company. For at least 10 years, there was no profit coming out of Amazon. They were in growth mode and all profits generated by the company have been reinvested. The company has grown bigger and bigger. Whilst in growth mode no dividends were paid out to investors or shareholders.

Bezos has built Amazon over the last ten tears to dominate the e-commerce and online shopping sector. Bezos knew this was a "winner takes all model": You are either the biggest e-commerce platform with all the logistics and the best customer service, or there are five other companies all trying hard with none of those companies really getting ahead. The industry would have remained fragmented with no one dominating or building critical mass.

With continual investment in the growth of the company, Bezos has built Amazon into a company that does dominate the sector; when you have the volume going through the warehouse and the delivery fleets, as well as a complete catalogue range for sale online, Amazon becomes the best choice for customers. If Amazon was not in such a position of dominance, the sector would have remained fragmented with none of the companies performing well. Amazon dominates and has set the standard for all other online retailers.

THE BENEFITS OF AMAZON FBA

Amazon is definitely a "winner takes all" company.

In order to get volume of sales, and to be the place where customers go to buy everything they need, Amazon need to be able to sell everything. They need customers to be able to buy exactly what they want, and the customer needs to receive exactly what they ordered.

Amazon is able to control the entireprocess of delivery to its customers. Amazon is able to guarantee exceptional customer service and speedy delivery, meeting and surpassing customers' expectations every time. Being able to guarantee customer satisfaction happens when Amazon controls the entire logistics process, from when an item is ordered, packed, leaves the warehouse, collected by the delivery driver, to when it is delivered to the customer.

This process is called "fulfilled by Amazon" or FBA. Rather than managing and shipping your own stock, which is time consuming and costly, and can't guarantee customer satisfaction as well as FBA, I recommend that you, as a third-party Amazon seller, use Amazon's Fulfilled by Amazon (FBA) services.

As a seller, you can piggyback on Amazon's incredible logistics process, its warehouses, even its reputation for providing amazing customer service and ensuring customer satisfaction.

GLOBAL DOMINATION

Amazon has spent a long time and a lot of money investing in other markets. The company has recently spent around $3 billion in India for example.

When the company expands into a new geographical location, or country, the entire platform is replicated, and over time, their entire catalog of products, including customer reviews. Amazon then starts shipping those products to customers around the world.

After incredible success in the US, Amazon then expanded

to Canada, the UK and then the rest of Europe.

Since those early years, Amazon has now opened in lots of countries: Japan, Australia, the Middle East, South Korea, Turkey, India..... Pretty much every developed country has some version of Amazon.

Some countries have adopted Amazon slowly, such as Australia where the company undertook a big launch. In other countries, they have had to jostle a bit with other e-commerce platforms; in India for example, Amazon has had to compete with KickStart. However. In other regions, Amazon really dominates and there is more potential for growth. Research suggests that there are 6 billion customers in Southeast Asia and South Asia who will be buying online.

Amazon is working hard to secure the majority share of that market.

Amazon is in a position where it can undertake long-term projects that are unprofitable, heavy on capital, heavy on investment in staff. These projects burn through the cash. It's a strategic move. Amazon is willing to make these huge investments in order to be in pole position when the time is right, and that market starts to take off. Buyers gain confidence to order everything they need on Amazon and the growth trajectory for Amazon in that country is exponential. Once this growth occurs, Amazon gains more customer confidence, volumes of sales increase and the venture becomes incredibly profitable.

It is very interesting to watch Amazon grow. It is fascinating to see how Amazon convinces its analysts and its investors to be patient, whilst waiting and believing in a bigger vision of a great future.

Jeff Bezos has shown time and time again that he is pushing all the boundaries. To give you an idea, Bezos is investing his own money in space research! He's definitely not working collaboratively with anyone else like NASA or Elon Musk on this venture, or any of his other ventures.

He is a very individualistic guy. He does his own thing with all his private wealth. He is an explorer, a builder and a big dreamer. And you can hitch your business to a company like Amazon easily.

Amazon is solid, established and is not going to disappear overnight. The company has developed reliable processes. Operationally speaking, Amazon is very solid.

There is no other company better to partner with as you grow your business.

100% CUSTOMER FOCUS

The Amazon customer experience is consistently good.

The policies that Amazon has in place are firmly customer focused and have been designed with the interests of the customer in mind. Existing Amazon sellers will know that the guidelines, policies and terms of business that sellers must agree to is in place to ensure that the customer experience is consistent and superior to Amazons competitors. Everything revolves around the customer experience.

If a "dodgy" or poor quality product is sent to Amazon to sell on to a customer, or we make certain claims about a product and Amazon then sells it to a customer, The Food and Drug Administration (FDA) will step in.

Amazon will always put measures in place that protect the customer. Amazon will not allow a product to be sold that makes false claims. It will not allow sellers to list products with banned ingredients, or ingredients not approved by agencies such as the FDA. Everything is in place to protect the customer.

If Amazon were to allow such products to be sold on its platform, this would have a negative impact on Amazon's brand and the customer experience. This is why the company is strict and why it requires sellers to sell quality products that meet all their requirements. Amazon needs to police who is selling what. When they do this at such a large scale, there are moments where it can be very frustrating as a seller. Occasionally, as a seller, you may experience double (or triple) checking of your products by Amazon, which can sometimes be a little frustrating.

During these frustrating times, it can be beneficial to understand how Amazon works, and the reasons behind some of their actions.

Protecting the safety and interest of their customers is paramount. Amazon will always put their customers first, and will put measures in place to protect its customers from a product that might not be safe, from a seller who might not be authentic or a review that might not be real.

Many customers will base their buying decisions on reviews of the products available on Amazon. As such Amazon has no tolerance for people tampering with reviews, product rankings, or product quality. In fact, in protecting the customer Amazon will not permit third party sellers to have contact with the customer at all. Sellers used to be able to email customers after each product order, which was great from a marketing point of view.

Now Amazon has really cracked down on reviews, and the sellers ability to request reviews for their products.

Until quite recently, sellers were able to follow up with customers directly and build a relationship. Sellers were once permitted to ask if they'd like to leave a review. Not anymore!

Now, Amazon protects their customers by letting them unsubscribe from all our emails that are hounding them after the sale. In fact, it is now against the company's terms of service for a seller to request a review from a customer.

PLAY BY THE RULES

In the recent review crack down, Amazon came down really hard on sellers who were manipulating the review system, and on sellers were "buying" fake reviews to make their listings lookgood.

Amazon clamped down on these practices because they are not considered to be in the spirit of the best customer experience. Some of the product launch tactics being used by Amazon sellers were not in the best interests the Amazon customer.

Amazon has introduced other, more legitimate ways for sellers to launch products proactively to curb manipulative practices, for instance Amazon loves people doing targeted pay per click advertising (more about that later). Amazon also favors those sellers who use their dedicated warehouses and delivery service because then they control the entire customer experience.

As a seller, if you are shipping a product to a customer yourself, and you have mistakenly misallocated your inventory, saying that the product is available whereas in fact it's not available, Amazon will penalize you heavily. Amazon does not tolerate this "sloppy" practice. Amazon will always give preferential treatment to the products that they sell using FBA, because they know that the customer experience can be controlled.

As stated, Amazon is a great platform to piggyback on for its volume, scale, reach plus the fact that customers trust them so much. Customers have their credit card loaded and they get free prime shipping within two days for that loyalty.

Customers can also choose same day delivery, and even get drone deliveries and same hour deliveries in some cities. There are amazing opportunities for your product by partnering with Amazon and selling on its platform.

It is undoubtedly the best e-Commerce platform from which to sell a product.

Not only is it convenient and profitable, it is also a real privilege to partner with Amazon to sell products to customers who are shopping online. Amazon is unrivalled. There is nowhere else like it on the internet or in business. Partnering with Amazon is, effectively, having access to all the world's customers. Your chosen products match what Amazon customers are looking for in categories where those demands are not adequately met.

From my experience, Amazon is a fantastic company to work with and can be considered as a true partnership. When we sell our products, Amazon makes money and we make money. Amazon supports its third-party sellers and the company wants to see us succeed.

It's a very good partnership from that financial point of view. However, as third- party sellers, we must ensure that we are only selling quality products. If we sell a bad quality product, Amazon will penalize us because they don't want their customers to experience a bad quality product.

This encourages good behavior from sellers. Unfortunately, when there is a lot of money to be made, some people choose to behave badly and take costly shortcuts. Amazon takes a hard stand on these operators which is ultimately good for genuine third-party sellers offering quality products. Every time Amazon introduces a policy change or closes down a loophole, its ultimately for the greater good.

These policy changes and loophole closures always works in my favor and for the students I coach, because we are doing things the right way: Creating real products or good quality with good price points that real Amazon customers will enjoy and want to buy more of.

Unscrupulous sellers who focus on tricking the system, rigging the rankings, buying reviews will always eventually come unstuck. Eventually Amazon will catch up with them and penalize them, sometimes closing down their listings and seller accounts completely.

It makes great business sense that Amazon is really hard on unscrupulous sellers because if they were not tough and didn't enforce these policies and rules, people (the customer) would not trust Amazon or the quality of the goods. Imagine if there were no safety standards or if the reviews were not real, Amazon would not have a business and customer confidence would be lacking.

Amazon has to uphold that trust by being tough. As a third-party private label seller, there are days when Amazon being tough can be annoying and slightly inconvenient. Overall though, we enjoy a robust business on Amazon because they take the safety and the regulatory considerations so seriously. This all comes back to the customer experience and Amazon's determination to provide the very best service for its customers.

Understanding how Amazon thinks can be a steep learning curve, and sometimes it can be frustrating when you deal with Amazon's customer service team as a seller. Ultimately though, if we understand that central to Amazons business model is customer satisfaction, everything about the company and how to best profit from partnering with Amazon makes sense.

DO THE RIGHT THING

Amazon has extensive support systems in place to help you as a third-party private label seller. Firstly, the dashboard issued to you as a seller is intuitive and self-explanatory, and easy to navigate. There are policies to read and agree to as a seller. You will have to spend time understanding what teams Amazon has on their seller support end to know where to direct your enquiry. Once you know the roadmap, your questions and queries can be dealt with quickly, efficiently and directly with Amazon staff.

Amazon will keep you closely updated on new protocol and policies associated with selling products on its platform. It is, of course, important to read the notifications that are posted on your seller support page. These notices help us a lot as sellers on Amazon. As sellers we are constantly up-skilling and being educated, and as a seller it's important to make sure you really understand the company that you are placing your products with and getting your customers from.

It is important to invest time in understanding how Amazon operates and how it "thinks". This will be time well spent and you will be better placed as a seller. You will soon understand that inconvenient policy changes are actually in our best interest as sellers. This understanding will ultimately help with your product selection.

In partnering with Amazon, you can take your products and brands right around the world. You can scale-up, you can diversify and even have subscription services running. There are amazing things available for the right sellers, with the right products, doing it the right way. But you must do it Amazon's way, or die trying! If you try and do it any other way, you will be fighting an uphill struggle to win on Amazon.

If, however you adopt the right mindset early on in your partnership with Amazon, the company will be delighted to have you there and will actually help you sell your products!

Onwards and Upwards

Here is a brief summary of my top tips for selling successfully on Amazon, and how best to develop an effective partnership with Amazon:

1. Spend the time exploring what makes Amazon tick.
2. Understand how does Jeff Bezos sees opportunities?
3. Understand how seller support teams get trained to deal with your challenges? How do you help them, help you?
4. Spend time developing the right vocabulary and open the case the right way, and use Amazons unique seller support service effectively. How to know when to be assertive and when to back off?

Mastering this will give you the best chance of seller success.

CHAPTER THREE

COMMON MISTAKES MADE BY AMAZON SELLERS

Over the last five years, I've spent a lot of contact time both online and in person, with hundreds of other Amazon sellers. It has been wonderful and I have learned a lot from them.

I have attended events, conferences and meet up groups. I have also got to know them through social media pages and getting to work with my own students.

It has been a real privilege over the last few years to have people taking my advice on how I choose, launch, and promote products on Amazon.

In many cases, I also eventually provide advice and support to help Amazon sellers, sell their whole business.

I've seen a lot of people do very well. I've also seen a lot of people get started and then, for various reasons, not take their business to its full potential.

I've seen a lot of people make mistakes.

I love going to a conference where somebody opens their presentation and shares some horror story about how they lost $12,000 in their first week on Amazon. They show great vulnerability when they inform us of their learning.

How do some sellers loose so much? Examples would include having a coupon code"go wrong" by not being set up correctly, or some get into major debt and end up with a hideous debt collecting agency coming after them, after overextending themselves financially to grow their Amazon business too fast. There are always terrible stories and they make everybody in the room cringe.

It is so easy to make mistakes when you are new and don't know what you're doing. You have not been taught how to do things the right way. More importantly, you have not had that experience to see all the things ahead of you and to know which is the right one to do.

There are a lot of forks in the road with an Amazon business. You have many choices.

Do I borrow money to invest in inventory, or do I go out of stock on a popular product?

Do I undertake a really aggressive launch campaign or go a bit slower and see if I can find customers a different way rather than a give away?

There are so many different opportunities that we come across: Different ways to choose our products, different ways to choose our suppliers and different ways to launch our products.

When it comes to the "nuts and bolts" elements of Amazon such as your listing, running advertising campaigns, running ongoing promotions with Amazon and managing your customers, there are a multitude of different ways to do things.

The biggest inflection point where people either get onto a good track that is ultimately successful versus a much harder or a bad track, really comes down to product selection.

I spent a lot of my time when I'm training my students, on what to do to have a "good run" with Amazon. 90% of what I teach is around clarity in choosing the right product. If you can choose a product that is low competition, you will avoid most of the horrors and pitfalls.

This is what selling a competitive product looks like: Expensive advertising, nasty tactics, difficulty getting people to find your product, difficulty winning the sale when there is cheaper products that are similar. As soon as you're selling a competitive product, life is difficult!

Similarly if you have a very low competition product, for example if you are the only one selling that product, you may have a challenge at the other end of the spectrum: Not that there's too many competitors, but that there is not enough customers. In this scenario, perhaps your product is too niche. Not enough eyeballs are going to land on your product listing each month, for you to be able to make the amount of sales that you need. There is always this eternal quest for the sweet spot in the middle to find the perfect product.

What I want to cover in this chapter, is to look at some of the most common mistakes I've seen people make as Amazon sellers, and how to avoid those pitfalls.

The single most important thing you can get right is choosing the right kind of product.

Understanding the criteria behind a winning product and knowing where to get your data from when you're doing your research is critical. Having really robust and clear ideas about why you are in business and where your brand is heading is also important. It is about building brands, not building individual products.

When you build a quality product that has a real point of difference, not a copycat product, then everything becomes easier. You have a point of difference that customers love to hear about. When you launch, you have a reason to influence customers to buy because there's actually something new.

When you want to charge a premium price, customers understand they are getting more than the inferior version offered by your competitors. Premium products are always the way to go, rather than trying to make your margin on cheap cost of goods.

With that background, I want to share some of the mistakes I see people make in their quest for the perfect product.

Everybody starts on Amazon with great ambitions. They want to generate passive income. They are often motivated by wanting to quit their day job or to be able to afford things they currently cannot. Maybe they want to have more time with family. More time for travel, and not being stuck in one location.

Starting out, the possibilities of what lies ahead is so liberating and exciting. We all start out on Amazon raring to go, excited about what's going to happen next.

Then we start doing some work.

Many sellers invest in a training program, so you've got some structure to follow. It's much easier to follow your way through the critical steps, to make sure you understand what is going on at each step.

Of course, there is always the risk of overwhelm, however there is no point having a blueprint that is as simple as "color by numbers" and so simplified that you haven't actually understood what matters when becoming an Amazon seller.

When I teach my students about Amazon, I ensure they understand how Amazon thinks.

We discuss what customers do to find your product and how Amazon's algorithms arrange the products. I teach how to get onto page one and look at how the promotions on Amazon work, including how your pricing strategy needs to work.

All this comes after you've chosen a great product, found a great supplier and completed all the shipping. There are lots of steps to the process.

Even when I break everything down and turn it into a step-by-step process for people, there are some that want to race ahead and do it all in a weekend. They are in a real hurry to find their first product and get started.

At the other end of the spectrum, there are people who never choose their first product because they just get frozen by being overwhelmed. They are unable to go step-by-step through the necessary work to do to do well on Amazon.

MISTAKE 1: GETTING STARTED

The first challenge I see that people face on Amazon, is not getting started. I see a lot of people become stuck here, comfortable in the endless world of procrastination.

I have been a member of some really big Facebook communities over the years and talked to thousands of people who sell on Amazon. Amongst the thousands who have started selling, there are tens of thousands who had that exact same, paid training access, the same books or podcasts that they could listen to and yet they don't get started. Ever.

In a few years, they will come to really kick themselves for having missed out on this big opportunity.

Amazon is still a huge opportunity. There is always somebody saying, "Oh, it was easier two years ago," but that's just business. There will always be change and there is often a first mover advantage. When people realize there is an opportunity on a marketplace, they start selling a product or a service.

Selling products on Amazon may become more mainstream

over time and profit margins may get tighter as more competition creeps in. But that doesn't mean that the opportunity is over. It means you have to choose a different type of product that's not quite so mainstream.

I used to sell big best-selling products. One day, I was actually number one in the entire health and personal care category on Amazon. I would never choose that type of product now, or one that would even have the potential to rank that highly today because there is so much competition in that space. The opportunity there has dried up, but there are amazing opportunities elsewhere on Amazon.

I like to stay under the radar, be a bit of a dark horse on Amazon, and do lots of lower volume, lower competition products.

A lot of people have all that same training. They've had it for years or maybe they just got it yesterday, and they just don't get started. You need to log in. You need to be somewhere you can sit quietly with your laptop and watch your training videos. Start your online product research.

There is a crucial step right at the beginning, which is opening your Amazon account. A lot of people never even open their Amazon account! When they do, they say, "Oh, I'll do the individual membership because I don't want to spend $50 a month," all because they are not ready to commit.

I recommend registering for professional account from the start and get ready to take this venture seriously. It is a huge opportunity and that $50 a month to register as a professional seller is a drop in the ocean financially when you look at what's ahead when you do thisright.

Starting by dabbling, dithering, sitting back and doing the least possible to get through it is not a great strategy to achieve success. It means you are not fully leaning in or fully committed to building your Amazon business as fast and aggressively as you can.

You want to jump at this, get momentum and keep that momentum going.

Often the people that don't open their Amazon account after watching the first training session, 'How to Set Up and Open your Amazon Account', are also the people that are not going to choose a product and are not going to choose the right supplier. Sadly, they may not do anything ever.

When you start this journey, you need to be very action-oriented. Make sure you are not one of these people that make this very common mistake of not getting started.

Amazon is a huge opportunity. There are millions of products being sold every day and you want to get amongst the action. The only way to get your product up is to start at the beginning, do the work, and get started.

There is a lot to learn on the way. It can feel overwhelming in the beginning. There are so many "unknowns", maybe an acronym being used you've never heard of. Maybe there's a member in your Facebook group who is constantly grumbling about something.

Some days, it can be hard. I get it because I've been in that position too. I've had days where I've thought this is a day where I'm just going to do something really easy. I'll just listen to a podcast or have a look for some new product ideas that I'll park and research, assess more thoroughly another day.

You don't need to do difficult stuff every day, but there are some steps where you really have to do them the right way. Such as opening your account or researching and finding that first product.

A lot of people will be really kicking themselves by not becoming Amazon millionaires, which they could have been had they just done those first few steps, opened an account and chosen the first product.

MISTAKE 2: LOOKING FOR "THE ONE"

The second biggest mistake I observe, are people that never get going on Amazon because they are waiting to find the perfect product.

Of course, we need to assess each product idea thoroughly, but the people who, as a generalization, tend to be very analytical can sometimes struggle to get going. Part of the reason for this is that they are focusing on the data to choose their products. There are many options of research tools that can assist with product selection and validation. When I started my Amazon journey, these tools didn't exist. Instead we analyzed everything on Amazon itself with a focus on rankings, reviews and the quality of the other listings.

Using the research tools can be an efficient use of your time as they are able to crunch and present a huge amount of data. However, as Amazon sellers it is critical not to be over reliant on the tools when undertaking product research.

For instance, some of the software tools will spit will generate an "opportunity score" such as, "This product is an eight out of 10, excellent idea," or "There's five other people making $1 million a month selling a product like this with this keyword."

There's a huge amount of data out there that is really opening up and making transparent what's currently happening on Amazon. For sellers on Amazon this is a great opportunity as you have so many more data points to gather before you hit go on your product. It is important to be cautious with the date presented by some of the software tools as it's not always accurate, but it's a start.

The process for selecting a product is quite straight-forward. First, you need to come up with a product idea. Then you need to identify the keywords that describe that product. You then need to check the numbers focusing on the level of demand (ideally this will be high) and the level of competition (ideally this will be low).

This is where many new sellers to Amazon come unstuck: They are searching for the perfect product. They are looking for really high demand but with virtually no competition and an amazing profit margin. Having launched over 500 products and researched thousands more I can categorically state that there is no product out there that is the perfect product!

So how do I identify a good (not perfect) product for Amazon? I have developed a checklist with pages of criteria and things that I have on my wish list for the perfect Amazon product. I have looked at thousands and thousands of products, and I have never found a product where I have been confident to say to myself, "Yes, that one's perfect."

It is simply not a reasonable expectation that a perfect product even exists. This can be extremely difficult for some people because they are waiting for the perfect product.

For EVERY product I've launched, I have had some niggles and some worry.

Is that competitor able to drop their price when I turn up?

Is that demand figure on that research tool accurate?

Is the supplier I've chosen going to be reliable?

Is the quality going to be good? You will always have unanswered questions until you get going.

Once you've got going, with your product listed on Amazon, there are some other questions you need to answer.

What's the best way to promote this?

Should I restock product A or launch product B?

There is always a challenge and a set of unanswered questions.

If you are waiting to find the perfect product, there's a danger that you will never actually get started selling on Amazon. Rather, you need to be prolific and willing to live with some imperfect data as you decide on your first product.

The way to get around making that mistake is to see your first product as a learning product. The process for selling on Amazon needs to be learned, and the best way to this is with a low risk, low cost first product launch.

Roger Hamilton, who is a smart businessman and educates a lot of entrepreneurs says, "If you're not earning, you're learning."

It is important that your first product is low cost, low risk and small quantities. Even though it may be tempting when you find a competitors product that seems to be selling well, don't order a container load of a brand new product that you have never sold before. Start small.

Make sure you have understood each step thoroughly as you have completed it.

It is also important to make sure you have researched your product over a number of weeks, not just in one day. You need to create a picture over time of what is happening on page one for that keyword.

Sometimes, you may want to even order a competitor's product. Or perhaps you have undertaken some more reading beyond Amazon to get a handle on different keywords for this product. Check out the different "chats" going on in social media and trends on Google for the product you're researching.

Despite undertaking considerable research, a perfect product is not likely to present itself.

Instead, at some point you are going to have to move out of your comfort zone and into action, with imperfect data. The conversation you have with yourself at this point may go something like this: "Right, this product is not perfect. The margin is not a full 30% but you know what? It's going to cost $1,000 to launch, the supplier has been really flexible and maybe, over time, the price can come up or the cost of goods can come down, but let's just get started."

Once you start to take action, you're learning and you will start to see the real data. You see what the advertising cost is going to be. You get a bill for the shipping fee and you know what the shipping actually is rather than an estimate. Actually launching that first product takes you away from theory and into practice.

There is so much to be said for "getting in the game". By being in the game you are more likely to find ten imperfect products to add to your Amazon business which enable you to refine your learning and get better and better at identifying profitable products. This is so much more effective than waiting for the unicorn perfect product, which may never appear.

One thing is for sure; If you don't go live with the product, your sales are zero, guaranteed.

Not getting started on Amazon is one of the most common mistakes I see in this business. When I coach people, I'm often coaching them through analysis paralysis!

These people have loads of data, but they just can't hit go because something is not perfect about the product. Perhaps there are too many competitors, not enough demand, the supplies aren't perfect, or they can't think of a really great point of difference. The product doesn't need to achieve a 10 out of 10 score to be a good product to sell on Amazon, and there are always going to be uncertainties. We want our product ideas to be perfect which will guarantee success, but that's not a realistic situation. Sometimes a product that achieves an 8/10 is good enough to be successful on Amazon.

We can compare the process of finding the perfect Amazon product to searching for a house to purchase: You are very unlikely to find a bargain house on the best street that no one else is bidding for. Each house you look at will not tick all the boxes, but if that house meets most of your criteria, that is good enough. You just have to start somewhere and improve on what you get, work on it, sacrifice a few things and compromise. The same mindset needs to be used when looking for your first product (and all subsequent products).

It's easy to sit on the sidelines your whole life and watch people who take imperfect action every day streak ahead just because they are in the game and playing the game, improving every day.

The mistakes I see from the students I coach, and others can be summarized into two points, and these two are interrelated:

Mistake number 1: Not getting started on Amazon
Mistake number 2: Waiting to find the perfect product

These are the two biggest mistakes I see, but there are others......

MISTAKE 3: IN SOFTWARE WE TRUST?

This mistake is also linked to mistake number 2: waiting for the perfect product.

I see an increasing number of people becoming increasingly reliant on software tools to do their product research, and that's fine, but only in moderation. There are some great tools out there to help people validate the product ideas. Here are some of the software tools:

1. **Helium 10**. Comprehensive suite of functions. Easy to use with reliable data

2. **Merchant Words**. Great for coming up with keywords and product ideas. The data can be variable.

3. **Jungle Scout** has recently upgraded is suite of functions and I have found its reports useful

There are many other tools out there and I critique these in my training. I also, and most importantly, show you exactly how I use those tools and how to read the data presented in the reports generated. In some cases the most effective way I use the tools is quite different from how they are actually designed to be used.

As a cautionary note, I would never use one of software research tools to generate product ideas for me!

Sometimes when I'm coaching Amazon sellers, I see waves of people coming to me with the exact same product ideas, asking me directly, "Do you think I could sell a spice rack?" or "Do you think I should sell weighted blankets? "Do you think I should sell macramé wall hangings?" The product ideas are all identical and they are often quite obscure products.

When this happens, I ask my student, "Where on earth did you get this idea from?" "Oh, Jungle Scout gave it an 8 out of 10," they reply, or "It came up number one as a product over $35 with not too many reviews on the competition and monthly revenue of x dollars. I plugged in my perfect list of criteria into the software tool, and this product popped out. I think it looks awesome."

There is a very dangerous trap with this as a strategy for finding your product. There are so many Amazon sellers, possibly hundreds of thousands. There are some very smart ones, aggressive ones, some with very deep pockets and big research teams, and they are all crawling through these software tools. They are looking for products that fit those exact same criteria that you're also researching.

When you base your research entirely on these tools, you come away with a number of product suggestions that have an "opportunity score". Indeed, the product generated appears to be a great opportunity. However, you can be pretty sure that a significant number of other people (sellers that might not show up on Amazon the day you do your competitor research) with the same product idea. In fact, you can be pretty sure that by the time your product is ordered, manufactured, shipped and landed, there may be 30 or 50 other people who are now selling the same product.

This scenario comes about because everyone has done the exact same product research using the same software tools at the exact time and who got the same type of training as you! It is a real fool's game to be over reliant on software tools and to take the numbers at face value.

Sometimes the data presented by the software tools do not make any sense. If an opportunity generated by a software tool looks too good to be true, it probably is.

If the data doesn't make sense, it probably isn't reliable and shouldn't be relied upon. There are lots of blips in the data and so it is essential to apply common sense, logic and think like a real human.

A successful seller on Amazon will develop strategies and principles that keep them away from the risks of an overly competitive marketplace, or they have strategies in place that ensure that they do not select overly competitive products to launch.

When presented with seemingly incredible data, step back and look at what you're being presented with a critical eye. Does it make sense that that product would really cost x dollars? This product is made by a Chinese supplier. They have only been selling for three months, yet they are doing $2 million a month in sales.

Does the data sound right, or too good to be true? The software tools are not clever enough to determine whether or not something is too good to be true, so we need to engage our brain.

As well as these research tools giving everybody the same idea on the same day, sometimes there are instances where unreliable data gets fed into the tools. This means you must not rely on the software tools, or the data that they generate to make your decisions.

The software tools can only tell us half the story about a product. There are other things those research tools cannot tell you. For instance, the tools cannot tell you that the top three sellers, who are doing a hundred thousand a month in revenue, are actually doing a mega give away with coupon codes!

Sometimes, sellers can use launch services in the background and these numbers are artificial sales and not a true indicator of their revenue. They might all be a 99% discount coupon codes.

Other tactics sellers use that may influence the numbers maybe that someone is running a Paypal rebate behind the scenes, whereby an overpriced sale goes through, paid for normally through Amazon, ensuring that the product is launched and ranked fast.

Or maybe somebody is running out of stock and they have dropped the price massively, they have ranked really high, but that was never their normal price.

Another scenario would be if a competitor is about to run out of stock and they have just jacked their prices up to slow down the sales.

Also, you do not know if a product is out of stock on Amazon.

The tool might not pick it up because the listings disappear from Amazon when they go out of stock. This is why you need to watch similar product sales for a while to get the full picture. The software tools can't show you this level of data granularity.

In the past, I have even looked for my own products on the research tools and they're simply not there. Whether my product is out of stock or in stock, the numbers look wrong on some of my products.

Research and software tools do have a useful place especially when wanting to compare different product opportunities side by side. As long as you understand the limitations of software tools and you use your brain to analyze the data you are presented with, sometimes it's helpful to work with hard numbers.

Of course, I like to refer to the research tools to validate my ideas. But I also like to look on Amazon and I base all my key decisions on what I'm seeing on Amazon. I like to check the FBA calculator is giving the same expense with Amazon FBA fees as a research tool.

I also like to look wider than both Amazon and the software tools when validating product ideas.

1. I like to check that the Facebook groups talking about this product are talking about trends, what's in, what's out, what new features the best products have, and I ensure that my product fits all the criteria: if my competitors are offering a 3inch version, but the Facebook groups are saying that a 7inch version would be better, then I develop a 7inch version. I strongly advise against simply copying a competitors' product with no point of difference and hoping to win on Amazon.

2. Another place I like to look to validate my product ideas is Google Trends. Here I like to investigate keyword trends, and where my potential product is most popular geographically.

3. I like to look on Pinterest and Etsy and see how other sellers have packaged and photographed similar products. From Pinterest and Etsy I often get great ideas for my point of difference.

4. The best place to base your research is always on Amazon.

Do I need a software tool?

Possibly not.

All the information we need is available on Amazon itself. You can see from the ranking what other Amazon sales people have made, theoretically, and multiplied their ranking equivalent number of units per day by the sale price to see their revenue. Then you can see from their price and once you have an idea for the cost of goods, you can see how much margin they are making.

The software tools simply make this process more efficient. But I cannot stress enough the importance of engaging your brain and a degree of common sense when analyzing the data you are presented with.

Once you have a very clear picture of the product, its competitors, what buyers are satisfied with in relation to that product, and how that product can be improved, then (and only then) you can fairly confidently move in.

Having done your research and knowing that your product is going into a space where there are five sellers generating

$10,000 USD a month, or more in sales and there may be an opportunity for you to corner reasonable proportion of that market with the launch of your (ideally superior) product.

My advice is to be very wary about relying on research tools for business decisions. It is one source of data points, only one of many. You need to build an accurate picture that tells the real story about the product you are about to launch in the market you are about to enter.

Don't be lazy. Be thorough. Product selection is an important decision and nobody cares about the success of your product more than you.

The actual algorithm that drives the research tools is merely crunching the business, spitting out numbers and words. There is no judgment or critical analysis at all.

Even the more advanced research tools, if they had artificial intelligence built in, do not (cannot) care about your business as much as you. The tools cannot read the quality of the listing as well as you can read the quality of the listing. They cannot interpret the reviews or identify an opportunity.

What the software tools can do is save you time, but it is not enough to rely on the data generated by itself and in isolation. My advice is to tread very carefully with your use of research tools and use it to validate your ideas. But those ideas must have checked out elsewhere.

Above all, do not use it to generate product ideas.

When you are validating your product ideas, make sure that you are looking at a few different places. Look online and in retail to come up with the best ver-

sion you possibly can of your product idea.

Check that there is enough activity going on enough sales and not too much competition. Use multiple places to double check everything looks as it should and aligned.

Once you are a more experienced seller and have been the process of researching a product and launching it on Amazon, you will start to notice what looks right and what looks wrong.

For instance, your critical eye will start to pick up on anomalies: Those FBA fees look way too low or, I'm surprised that's not in the oversized category given that it's a large and heavy arm chair.

Malcolm Gladwell's book teaches how some people are drawn to the details or can spot anomalies instinctively, whilst others need to spend time working through a process not just once, but hundreds of times to wire the brain to think differently and begin to spot patterns. He estimates that the brain has been retrained only when a person has completed 10,000 hours of working on a particular way of thinking. This is when you really master a subject and you start to achieve a level that expertise. It then becomes wired into your brain.

Having worked on my own Amazon business for 5 years, and having researched thousands, and launched hundreds of products, I am now in a position where I can recognize anomalies quickly. I can also recognize promising product opportunity. Five years into selling on Amazon, my instincts about products are usually reliable, more reliable than thedata.

Early on in my Amazon journey, I had to choose my products by sitting and doing hours and hours of research: looking at the data, comparing all the pros and cons of different products and making a decision on each product idea based on my analysis of the data and information I was presented with.

Later on, those ideas started to come to me more organically: With time you will develop sophisticated methods of analyzing data, you will also have a deeper understanding of the market, and you will find that you cringe when you see just how wrong some of those numbers are in the research tools! You know they are wrong, but somebody new to Amazon and over-reliant on the research tools could potentially fall into a real trap if they took those numbers at face value.

My advice is to never be overly reliant on research tools. They are great and they do have a place, but they are not the only consideration when looking to choose your product.

MISTAKE 4: BRIGHT SHINY OBJECTS

Another mistake I see people making is, getting distracted by other business opportunities that promise big returns for relatively little investment of time and money.

It seems that there's a guru around every corner offering to teach us the secret of their success, all wrapped up in a convenient online course. I am bombarded with courses on Shopify, how to be a social media influencer, how to drop ship, how to run Facebook advertisements to promote your product, here's another Amazon course that is better than all the other Amazon courses.

Shiny object syndrome is very real with each new business opportunity looking more attractive, and potentially, easier than the last. Things can sometimes look easier and better than the way you are doing it right now. The grass is always greener and the marketers are very smart.

As a new Amazon seller you are doing your homework, researching many different options before deciding on your first great product idea.

You launch that product and sales are slow. We may be inclined to think we have missed something, or listed the product incorrectly, and our doubts are suddenly met with somebody turning up saying,

- "Oh, let me rank your product for you. It would only cost you a few thousand dollars."
- "What you really need is a Shopify site; Let me set up a Shopify site for you."
- "Let me do email marketing." "Let me run Facebook ads for you." "Let me teach you how to run Facebook ads for you."

Suddenly, we are inundated with a multitude of highly appealing, sometimes too good to be true sounding offers to improve our business, or our product sales.

Some of these offers are legitimate and do have a place. However, consider them for a more advanced Amazon seller. The first year of your Amazon business is all about getting the basics right. Only after that will you be in a position to know exactly where we need to put our resources, where to invest some money, and what tasks of the business need to be outsourced.

Keep your eyes on the Prize!

When you are starting out, do not get distracted.

When you start your Amazon journey, your first year should be all about learning the basics about selling successfully on Amazon. Getting distracted away from this focus is another really common mistake I see people new to Amazon make.

People get distracted with the topics that other people are talking about, and there's nowhere worse for this type of distracting "noise" than in social media groups.

Facebook pages dedicated to Amazon seller communities can be wildly distracting, and take us away from our focus. People start chatting add-ons to their Amazon businesses that are not necessary when you first start out (and focusing on this when you start out can be distracting).

For instance, people get consumed with the latest add-on, research tool or follow- up software. People talk about things like chat bots, which can be nice to have, but only when your business is established and your products selling well.

As well as selling, its important to first get some customer loyalty and then you've got something to do later when you've got a nice database. But, before you have a dozen products selling well, my advice is to not worry about marketing beyond

Amazon. And that's the beauty of starting out on Amazon: it already has customers searching for your product with high intent to buy.

There is no other place online where you get this: free traffic and a high conversion rate.

A high percentage of people who see your listing on Amazon then go onto buy your product. The conversion rate on Amazon is much higher than on other ecommerce sites such as Shopify.

Similarly, when you commit to a private labeling business model, you are rewarded with high profit margins that are generally better than the drop shipping profit margins.

A drop shipping business can look extremely attractive when you are facing big product bills in your private label business, but my advice is to stick with private labeling, as it is the model where you make the most margin, where you can control your product and where you can sell your brand for a premium price one day.

Getting back to the danger of shiny objects, only when your business is established should you start to think about how you can diversify onto different platforms or sales channels.

All these distractions will be waved in front of you. They appear golden and shiny, highly attractive and a fail safe ticket to commercial success. **But there is no better place to be selling than on Amazon.**

In fact, and most importantly, there is no better skill to get good at than choosing Amazon products.

You can outsource many elements of your business down the track, but if there is one thing to get good at, to be profitable and successful with this online business, it would be learning how to choose good Amazon products.

Maybe one day, you will diversify into other platforms successfully too. But do one thing well, do some work on it every day and complete it. Do not let it linger and don't jump, chop and change between 50 different training courses and shiny temptations.

Stick with one philosophy, follow it properly, follow people who have had good results. Get your results by doing what works rather than by half-starting ten things and switching when it gets too challenging.

Dedicate your efforts and resources to one methodology, and really commit. Learn everything there is to learn about that method, develop your own skills and expertise. Avoid the mistakes that I see so many people make.

MISTAKE 5: IS FACEBOOK REALLY YOUR FRIEND?

The next and final common mistake that I see people making is spending too much time on social media!

I have a dedicated and focused Facebook group for my own community and I'm a member of a number of other Facebook groups, but I rarely use it. I try never to check in as ahabit.

I prioritize engagement with my own Amazon community, but I never turn to Facebook if I want an important answer to an important question about the future of my business..

Unfortunately, the wisdom of the crowd does not prevail. There are many people who are not experts in this field. In fact they actually know nothing. They are not busy with their own business because they have not got their own successful business. Instead they are frequenting these groups offering unhelpful and misleading advice.

Unfortunately, they tend to stir and waste time because they are either procrastinating themselves, or trying to promote something else. Many of the answers offered by such people to the questions posed are often misleading, and more often simply wrong.

Within such groups, there is very little quality control, and there is a lot of noise to cut through: the one or two nuggets of useful information gleaned might have taken you considerable time to reach: you may have to sift a thousand other bits of useless content before you found that one useful piece of advice or wisdom.

Even worse, you might miss the useful accurate information entirely, and instead have your mind filled with conflicting information and advice. As such my advice is to avoid these Facebookgroups.

Feeling isolated: It can be lonely and isolating when you start an online business especially as your friends and family don't yet get what you're doing or understand the challenges you face. Despite this, in the same way I advise avoiding distracting Facebook groups, I also advise that you avoid approaching friends and family for advice about how to run your Amazon business.

Some of the conversations in the Facebook group have the best intentions. They are all about people supporting each other and offering motivation and encouragement especially when somebody has achieved some good results. A nice kind word when someone had a rough day can feel incredibly supportive.

Sometimes though, things can go too far the other way. Somebody starts to mope and feel a bit sorry for themselves and then, the rest of the group's mood changes and everybody sees the darkness and the sky is falling. It is all doom and gloom. Suddenly a small Amazon policy change means it is all over for all of us!

The tone and mood within these groups can be extreme: incredibly positive and supportive, or there can be an overly fatalistic negative undertone.

Sometimes I see people posting screenshots of huge sales days. There has been occasion where these same people approach me not long after saying, "I'm running at a big loss. My revenue's great, but I'm hemorrhaging cash because I've been doing all these promotions to get the sales."

The key message here is don't always believe what you see.

People will often only present a snapshot of their business in a favorable light. We have no idea what sits behind that business, what they're selling, how long they have been established, and what marketing strategies they have in place. In short, it's not our business, and should not distract us.

Alternatively, other people will turn to social media to vent about a problem that we have limited information about. Again, it's their business and should not distract you from your focus on your own business. This is not the energy you should be picking up on.

Your primary focus is to get your business up and running. Do not get distracted away from this.

Personally, I don't like Facebook groups. I choose not to participate in many. Facebook groups and social media takes time away from what we should be focusing upon. Many people lose so much time to social media groups getting the wrong content and misleading information whilst developing the wrong mindset. It's a huge distraction. This is not quality networking.

Good Amazon sellers tend to keep their products confidential. They also refrain from sharing exact product specifics. Sharing such information within a big group is very smart, and doesn't guarantee good advice. Even well meaning people cannot give good advice on a particular challenge you have because they don't know the full details.

The smartest sellers that I know are not in Facebook groups. They are doing their own thing quietly.

The smart sellers might have a training course where they share their best stuff, or a small circle of trusted people, but they're not giving the great stuff out in a Facebook group. They are not spending all day doing free YouTube webinars. They are not wasting their precious time. They are doing their own work with a razor sharp focus on building a successful and sustainable business.

For you to succeed in your Amazon business you need to access to the right people who support your journey. Surrounding yourself with the right people is invaluable and you should be prepared to pay for that. Don't be afraid to pay for the right expertise as the valuable advice you receive will pay dividends in the long term.

Unregulated and poorly moderated Facebook groups are not the place to get reliable business critical information. Your business is too important and your time too valuable to be given misleading information. If you base business critical decisions on the wrong information, the result could be costly, or in extreme situations, catastrophic.

Be very careful how you spend your time and where you source your information.

For most of us running an Amazon business, we have other commitments. We might still have a day job. We might have family. We might have other things that fill our days. Our time is an extremely precious resource. Use your time wisely and productively.

Establishing and building an Amazon business can sometimes be quite isolating and lonely. You need to be a self-starter and be comfortable with your own company. In this context social media groups and Facebook can be valuable to make new friends with people who share the same journey, and connecting with likeminded people. Facebook communities have limitations and should not be turned to for technical questions. If you are using Facebook to connect with people I urge you to limit the time you spend on social media.

You are better advised to spend an hour or two on your Amazon product research instead of scrolling through Facebook as this will give you a very different end results a year later!

Don't lose sight of what is possible when you are doing Amazon well. This will help you decide where best to spend your time. The time you have spent on social media could have been spent on finding and launching new Amazon products: you could have launched five new products, and that could equate to a $1million income stream!

The fastest way to get good at Amazon is to use your time wisely and not spend hours and hours scrolling through social media.

SUMMARY OF THE 5 MISTAKES TO AVOID

1. Not getting started on Amazon.
2. Waiting to find the perfect product, which does not exist.
3. Becoming overly reliant on software tools to choose or validate products.

4. Getting distracted by shiny object

5. Misusing your most valuable resource: Time. Spending too much time on social media.

Now you know the common mistakes people make when starting their Amazon journey, you can recognize them easily and put measures in place to avoid them.

If you notice yourself spending too much time looking for a perfect product, or you notice that you have bought four courses this month and still haven't finished your Amazon project, you will now be able to recognize that you may be falling into the trap of the common mistakes I see people making when starting their Amazon journey.

Per severe and remain focused on the things that really make a difference to your business's bottom line. The elements of the business that adds to your profit line in your business are where to invest your time.

Watch out for these mistakes and make sure you catch yourself early. If you see yourself starting to make any of those mistakes, pull out and be grateful that you have just saved yourself a potentially huge amount of previous time and money.

Focus on product research and get those products launched on Amazon and selling successfully.

Then you too can be a successful Amazon seller.

CHAPTER FOUR

AN INTERVIEW WITH SOPHIE HOWARD SUCCESSFUL AMAZON SELLER

HOW A BUSY MUM OF 2 CRACKED 7 FIGURES ON AMAZON AN INTERVIEW WITH SOPHIE HOWARD

Recently, I was interviewed about my Amazon system, so I thought I'd share it with you because it contains some useful insights for you. You can either read the interview below, or If you'd prefer to watch the video go copy and paste the link below into your browser:

https://www.youtube.com/watch?v=bYJtTfIoRUQ

Interviewer: Sophie Howard is a superstar Amazon seller. She's sold well over 500 different products on Amazon. She's made hundreds of thousands, in fact, millions of dollars of income. She's sold Amazon businesses, so she's a genuine world-class expert, and we're lucky enough to have here with us today. Thanks so much Sophie.

Sophie Howard: Yeah, I just love sharing with people what's working on Amazon today. I've had a lot of experience launching a lot of products, and I've really, really enjoyed the ride, the adventure of sourcing products from all around the world to sell on Amazon all around the world.

So whereas most people go for very obvious products, they're looking for where there's somebody already making lots and lots of sales and trying to piggy backing on that activity, I like to go where nobody else has.

I like to be under the radar with non-obvious products where I'm going to make profits. I am never impressed by other sellers sales revenue numbers. I am only interested in the profit that you get to take home.

The more competitive the product on Amazon, the less profit there is there for the taking. So a lot of my products have got virtually zero competition.

The day I launch, I'm at the top of page one, and I don't mind that it's slightly lower volume. There are plenty of customers out there on Amazon shopping.

Sophie Howard: So there's a bunch of criteria around the product and they really, really matter. I've got about eight pages of things I look for or things I make sure I definitely avoid when I'm choosing a product.

There have been some expensive mistakes when I haven't known something, and then being caught out, and I can help other people avoid making those same mistakes.

There are some particular categories, some niches, and some types of products where I see really low competition and where I can help other people make great profits selling in those categories.

Things like consumable products and products that are gifts are great. Just the numbers work so much better on those products.

If you want to do yoga mats, or supplements, it's going to be a pretty tough gig and it's one I don't want to play in, so I just teach people exactly what I do.

And I've launched well have over 500, probably nearly 1,000 different products on Amazon now.

Everything I've figured out that it's working, I teach. And I don't leave anything out when I teach. It's exactly what I do myself.

Interviewer: So basically, if a product's a big winner, then you add the criteria of that to your checklist, and if it's a flop, you can make sure you don't put it on the checklist, don't make that mistake. With that checklist and the system, you're learning from the experience of launching up to 1,000 different products, which is really valuable.

And I know as well as that you've also got a training course, which helps guide people step by step.

Sophie Howard: Yeah. There are a lot of Amazon courses out there. Most are prerecorded videos. That's fine. It might teach someone on the basics, but what I do is teach live everyweek.

I'm running my own Amazon accounts, so I'm always launching my own products. I'm always hearing from the rest of my students as well, what they're finding and learning and sharing. We've got a really nice community, which keeps us all up to date and current.

I'm doing my own testing and learning and selling, which keep me current, and I share that in a live coaching session once a week.

I also do some live teaching, and I've got a bunch of other coaches that help me answer all the questions that come in from the community. I answer those as well myself, if something's popping up that we have not come across before and so, it's always kept up to date.

It's always current and based on what's actually working, not what was a year or so ago. This is because Amazon's dynamic and the other tactics that I see people try sometimes work but they come and go.

It's a real trap to think that those "hacks" to beat Amazon at its own game are a smart strategy.

There are a lot of people promising that this fancy bit of software's going to spit out a $1 million product idea for you, and it is just nonsense. There's no way a decision that's that important to you should be trusted to a bit of toolkit that's not based on actual data.

Amazon doesn't release all that data, and there are a lot softer things in the decision-making around your product that I just don't see the software tools doing the right way for you.

So for example, there are software tools that give an opportunity score to a product, and when I look at that opportunity myself that they've given a really high score to, it's actually a terrible, terrible product that is doomed to fail.

Yet, people who don't know better are just following those bits of software, or some really fixed rules about what to do on Amazon and they just don't work because it's too dumbed down.

You need to actually do a little bit of work, maybe only 10 hours per product, but then you can feel really confident you've done your research right. The product's good and the supplier also good, and the way you're going to launch is completely within Amazon's terms of service.

This is a lot of gray area stuff being taught that I know Amazon doesn't like and people might get away with it short term, but I would never want to risk my million dollar Amazon asset for the sake of a quick way to try and trick the system.

So, play it really straight and look for really profitable long-term products.

Interviewer: Well that's right. Let's assume that the founders of a trillion dollar company are smarter than you, and they can work out ways to stop you in your nefarious scheme. So just try to do things the right way rather than try and be a 'black hat' seller.

A lot of people find having that coach to bounce their product ideas off very helpful. And yes, the coaches will evaluate the ideas with software, but they will also run it through the rest of their criteria as well, which I think makes such a big difference in launching products.

So, assuming someone was to start with your training academy, if they were a super eager beaver, how quickly could they potentially launch a product, and what's more of an average time to launch a product?

Sophie Howard: Good question. So my fastest student,

who's a lovey guy in Sydney, he was four weeks from hearing about Amazon to getting his product selling.

That's about as fast as you can do it. I was seven weeks. And then more typical, for somebody who's got a day job, family commitments, and other stuff on in life, I think maybe three months is a good average rule of thumb - because you don't want to go flat out and then feel overwhelmed.

You want to follow the way the program is structured because it's structured to help you succeed. What to do is watch one video and do one step at a time. Don't try and watch all the training and then try and remember what video 1 told you to do.

The biggest decision's the product. If you get that wrong, it doesn't matter what you do downstream, it's not going to work. So, book in calls with the experienced Amazon coaches, they're based all around the world.

We can fit in with time zones, lots in Australia and New Zealand, UK and US. We've got really experienced Amazon sellers who I've hand picked and I've gotten to know and trust them. They know me and how I teach, and we can help any student get some one-on-one personalized feedback with their products.

That's a real point of difference as well. It means somebody who's experienced and cares about your results is going to give you some personalized feedback.

Every product is different. So, there's some data, but there's also the value of experience, and I think the experience is what really sets this program apart. We've got people sharing to help you succeed.

Interviewer: I think that's so great. I know all these coaches, and one of them; for example, last year sold 30,000 units of a particular product. He's in the top 500 of the baby category on Amazon, which is an incredible achievement. He has a seven-figure business and to have someone like that on your team, personally mentoring and coaching you through the process of launching a product is worth its weight in gold, and that's something I haven't seen in the other courses, certainly in the price range that your course is offered. So, that's amazing. Tell me, Sophie how much would you budget to start off an Amazon business?

Sophie Howard: So, I hear horror stories of what people have spent launching their first product when they don't even know really what they're meant to be doing to find the first product.

Interviewer: Just buying a big container load of stuff from China.

Sophie Howard: Yeah, that makes me cringe and shudder, and it's such a waste of money, and it's such an awful thing to see happen when there's a much smarter way, which is to negotiate really small orders and really form partnerships with your suppliers.

I see a lot of people approach their suppliers all wrong, ask all the wrong questions, and not know which important stuff to check for. When that happens, you can waste a lot of money on a product.

My first product costs $300 to launch, and that product is still selling well. But maybe allow a thousand or a couple of thousand dollars and you'll be up and away with the product research really thoroughly and get it shipped. If you've got great packaging, it looks great in the images and in all the ways it's presented online.

So, doing a really classy, quality job for a product that you can charge a premium price for should be easily under $2,000 - $3,000 and you may invest some money into learning the skills. There's the $40 or $50 to Amazon every month, which you only need to pay once you start selling an a few other costs – such as company set up, if that's appropriate for you.

The model with Amazon's neat because you only really pick up the commission fees as you make sales, you don't have to hold any overheads and carry that cost yourself. Amazon is also incentivized to help you sell your products. So they only make money when you make money, which is great.

Their fees are very fair and very low, considering the access you get to their customers and their entire infrastructure. So yeah, it's all quite low cost.

Interviewer: The way I look at it is imagine if you could have a shop or a lease in an incredibly busy shopping center, but without paying thousands of dollars per month for rent, instead you're paying as little as around $50 per month. So, it's actually quite incredible to be able to get access to the biggest ecommerce site in the world for such a small investment.

But the reason for it is that when you sell well on Amazon, they make money. Around 50% of their revenue is from third party sellers, so it's quite an incredible opportunity.

Sophie Howard: And I think one of the other interesting things that is also a point of difference in the program is being able to sell these Amazon businesses.

So, I've sold a couple and everybody I teach, I teach them

that system from the beginning. You can't turn up with a box of receipts two years later, or a bunch of jumbled finances, or you haven't put the right contracts or agreements in place with your suppliers or some of the stuff around the product selection even makes a real difference to the valuation, you can get for your business later.

Teaching that process from the beginning is usually the best practice for your business being profitable and well managed. But just to have all that ready to go, if you ever did want to sell, then it's already there, sitting to be valued and you can sell that for a big lump sum.

That's something we teach in the program, and I don't know anyone else, certainly no one else in Australia sold a business like the Amazon ones I've sold.

One of my students who's actually one of the coaches, she's just sold her Amazon business for six figures and another coach is about to sell a seven figure Amazon business.

Interviewer: Wow. That is exciting, and it is so amazing just to be able to bring that income forward into one big payday because it can help set up your retirement, it can help pay for a mortgage, so working towards that is certainly a worthy goal.

Sophie Howard: And then there are other models on Amazon as well. I love the private label. It's got the best margins. But there are other ways to sell products on Amazon too. For example, you can partner with another company who's got an existing bunch of products, they don't know about Amazon and you've just learned these skills so you can help them and charge either as a consultant or do a profit share with another business that's got products that they want selling on the world's biggest platform.

Interviewer: And that's what you did when you started out, isn't it?

Sophie Howard: Yeah.

Interviewer: So how could that happen? You were selling on Amazon, and then it was babies' style products that you approached? Was it because you had little kids at the time?

Sophie Howard: Yeah, it was baby products because I had kids at home and a baby at home, and I was selling my own Amazon products pretty successfully. I was only a few months in, but had learned the ropes on Amazon.

I think it's important just to get stuck in and get started with your own first product quite quickly. Once you know what you're doing, it's the same process for all products.

I went out and found a bunch of local businesses that had great products and they weren't on Amazon. They were in New Zealand, probably didn't even know what Amazon was or how it could be possible for their products online.

I took their products and helped them set up their account and got that product selling on Amazon. For some of those companies, it's now the biggest source of income.

Interviewer: Wow.

Sophie Howard: And they charge more per product than they make at home selling it in their home country. So that's one model.

There's also going out there to buy another existing brand in bulk and reselling that. The margins aren't quite as good, but you do have that nice advantage through what's called drop shipping or wholesaling, that you don't need to invest in the product yourself up front. The margins aren't as good, but it's a very low barrier to get started. And it can be quite fun because you can have conversations with other companies, go there with a script, a bunch of questions, that product meets the criteria for wholesaling or drop shipping.

We teach you how to do that also because that can be a really nice quick way to get started nice and fast. Get your account up and learn the ropes on another product that doesn't cost you a lot to launch.

Interviewer: Yeah. Well, because you're starting off with zero stock. So just going back to it, you approached four companies and they said, yes. How much did you charge them per month to manage their account?

Sophie Howard: I charged $1,500 per month per client, and I got four of them.

I had four conversations, and I got four yeses because this was a no brainer for them.

It was like they had to put up a little tiny bit of stock, I would do all the leg work, it would be their own Amazon accounts that they would always own and if it worked, it could potentially be the biggest source of income and for some of them it was.

I learned a lot in the process. It was really good fun. It didn't take me a lot of extra time and I was using new skills. I wanted to sharpen up anyway, and so I got more experience, learned a lot and made some extra income.

Interviewer: Great.

Sophie Howard: After that monthly retainer, In the end, I switched to being commission based because I was helping themselves so much product and it was great for them and it was great for me. It helped diversify just from my own Amazon account as well.

So when I left my day job, I knew I had my Amazon product income, but I was also selling my services as an Amazon consultant, and that was a really nice back stoppage. And, of course, there are contracts in place and that replaced my salary on its own.

Interviewer: It's so amazing. And that's one of the great things about learning Amazon, because there are so many threats to normal jobs with the rise of robots and AI.

But one of the areas that is booming and growing is ecommerce. Having the skills around ecommerce and selling on Amazon and drop shipping makes have a very valuable high-income skill, which demands a lot of money in the market place.

So, to be able to earn maybe $6,000 a month from selling other people's products, as well as your income from your Amazon products is quite exceptional.

In Sophie's course, there's also a complete training program on how to do that, how to create an income selling other people's products and she's got her samples of the agreements that she uses and stuff. So, that's really great.

Sophie Howard: Yup. It's been good fun doing that. It's been interesting because you can do a lot of this work online, but then you get to help local businesses and see them succeed as exporters.

And before Amazon, if those companies wanted to export, they'd have to go and set up an international business and they'd have to pay tax in the states and they'd have to do all their banking in the states and employee stuff overseas and all their running costs. It would be a really expensive exercise with very uncertain returns.

But with Amazon, if I can help those companies present their products the best possible way on Amazon, they just send their stock and I do everything else for them.

I make some money, but they have this huge shot at hitting the biggest market on the world's biggest platform. And there's always going to be real people buying real things, and Amazon's the platform where they're all going to do that shopping.

Interviewer: Well, that's certainly been the case, and looks like it will continue to be the case. One of the things people say is they say, "I don't like Amazon because it puts, local main street shops at risk.

"To be honest, it does. But on the other hand, whether you're in Australia or New Zealand or Britain, think of all the entrepreneurs who are now able to get their products to a global market through Amazon.

I'm currently selling in America, and I'm just an average guy from the suburbs, and yet I've got a product selling the America. Now, 30 years ago if I wanted to do that, it would have been incredibly challenging. So, Amazon really does provide a leg up for local entrepreneurs who want to harness it. There's always a flip side to that coin, I think.

Sophie Howard: Yeah. A great chance for somebody to start their first business because you only really need to do one thing right, which is choose a profitable product.

Interviewer: Correct.

Sophie Howard: You don't need to do all the warehousing or customer service or sales teams or learn how to run Facebook ads. With lots of the other businesses that youcould start yourself online, you've got lots of different skills, lots of moving parts and lots of overheads, so there's virtually no overhead.

Under a hundred dollars a month with the Amazon fees, and then your skill, getting good at choosing the right products that are a fit for Amazon customers and presenting them well is all you need to do. Amazon does all the heavy lifting.

Interviewer: Once you've got the product in the Amazon warehouse with the FBA Fulfilled By Amazon service, they ship the product to the customers for you and they handle customer care and refunds, etc. That makes it a very hand through business. You've just launched your third brand, how long does it take you per day to manage your brand?

Sophie Howard: Minutes.

Interviewer: Minutes. Yeah.

Sophie Howard: I'm on my phone a lot of the time. I'm traveling at the moment, so I'll just keep an eye on sales on my phone, I'll keep an eye on messages on my phone. I can ping back a one liner if I ever need to. But really once a week I'll take a closer look at the sales and the stock levels, see what needs reordering, if I've got something flying off the shelves, I might do a sea shipment. So once a week, I look atstock.

Every day I'll just keep an eye on sales. Everything's looking healthy and normal. Nothing's going out of stock or anything. Then, once a month, I'll do an inventory assessment, just to check which products have been the most profitable, which ones are selling the most volume, how do I want to adjust the portfolio, what am I going to launch next. It's really easy.

Day to day, there's virtually nothing to do. If I'm launching a new product, I just follow the steps in the process, and it is very easy. I don't go in for these really big aggressive launches that run at a huge loss to trick Amazon. I think that's just daft, and you don't need to do it for the right kind of product. So I see a lot of people wasting money and time doing these great big launches for products that in the long-term won't be profitable.

So I do a low key launch and a low competition product, and then once a week check the key stats, there's some metrics around traffic, number of customers, the percentage that are buying, just checking that looks healthy. That can be 30% or more on an Amazon product.

Interviewer: Incredible.

Sophie Howard: And on your own website you'd be lucky to get 3% conversion so, great conversion rates because customers are ready to buy if you've got a product that's selling like hotcakes.

My worst problem is I can't stay in stock. I have to keep rushing these orders through to keep my suppliers keeping up. It's just that juggling act of new products I know will sell versus keeping in stock of the ones that are already selling.

Interviewer: So, realistically, it's less than 30 minutes a day, but the key thing is just keeping in stock of those products, which really does mean that this is the ultimate hands free business. People talk about the four-hour Work week and Tim Ferris obviously wrote the book about it, and a lot of people think it's completely unrealistic. But for an Amazon seller, it isn't unrealistic. You're going to put in more time than that when you're picking a new product and getting things organized, but once you've got a few products up and selling, it's realistic.

Sophie Howard: I've done this with a part-time job working for government, a four-month old baby and a toddler when I got started. So I was pretty sleep deprived.

Interviewer: A lot of us commute as well.

Sophie Howard: …And very short on budget. So I used to have a 20-minute commute on a bus, and I would do all my Amazon business off my phone on the bus.

Interviewer: Amazing.

Sophie Howard: And then I'd be at work, give that my full attention at the day, come home, and spend the evening with the kids. Once the kids were done for sleeping at night, I would do a little bit more work but it was never more than half an hour a day.

Interviewer: And you had big paydays while you were at work, when Amazon would do a promotion of your products, and you were making more from Amazon than you were at work.

Sophie Howard: Oh, way more. I had a day when I was at work, and I kept an eye on my phone during the day. I would hit refresh on the sales app, and one day I had made 33,000 US dollars while I was at work working for the New Zealand government.

Interviewer: So that's at least $10k in profit.

Sophie Howard: Yeah, 10,000 US profit. So that's probably about 14,000 to 15,000 New Zealand profit in a day.

Interviewer: That'll be like two months of work.

Sophie Howard: Or more for me because I was part time, so it was a total game changer. I stayed at work nine months after starting the Amazon business.

I was worried and quite risk averse. I was worried that it was beginner's luck or it was too good to be true, this can't last. But for five years now, every two weeks I've had an email from Amazon, "You're payment is on its way," and that's brilliant.

Interviewer: What would you say in net profit you'd want to be making off your Amazon product before you think about quitting your day job? I know it's different for each person, but just for you, what would that be?

Sophie Howard: Well, I didn't need very much because I was working part-time and paying a nanny to look after the children. So by the time I backed the expenses out, I didn't need to make more than, $5,000. I would've been happy to give up the day job if I felt really secure with it. But I was doing $50, $60,000 in the first few months, so I really got ahead.

Then I picked up those extra clients just to give me some certainty that this was a service I could offer as well as selling my products, and then I've never looked back.

And I don't wish I had left sooner because it meant by staying at work for that next six months or so after I'd got up and running, I was able to reinvest all those profits into more products.

Interviewer: Yeah. That's how you launched so many products.

Sophie Howard: Yeah. So, I never got into debt. I never maxed out credit cards and never borrowed to grow my business. That first business that did 1.6 million in the first year or so in sales was all grown through profits.

Interviewer: That's so amazing because most people, or a lot of people with their businesses certainly, they borrow money against the house or from friends and foes and family or venture capitalists or whoever to get things started, and that just puts your business on that back foot.

It is helpful to have money, but you've always got that back foot and you've got to pay back that debt, whereas in Amazon business, if you can start with low test runs of products. I'm personally investing about a thousand dollars on two different products to test at the moment. That's not a lot of money to test two products on Amazon. So it is a unique in the sense that you can self-fund a big empire.

Sophie Howard: It gives you real scale, but also lifestyle. When I started, I looked at all sorts of different business models.

Could I do multilevel marketing from home?

A lot of my other mom friends were doing a bit of that, but it looked really hard work and a long game and very uncertain what you'd actually get back for the time put in and a big time commitment.

Interviewer: It doesn't suit everyone to be selling stuff to their friends.

Sophie Howard: No.

Interviewer: For some people it comes naturally, but some people regret having awkward conversations with all their friends.

Sophie Howard: Totally. It makes my toes curl thinking about it. As much as I need some Tupperware myself, I can see that hosting a Tupperware party would backfire.

Interviewer: It's not for everyone.

One of the things at Amazon is you're selling a lot of staff, but you don't ever have to have a sales conversation. In fact, you don't even ever need to post one single product because Amazon handles so much of that for you. So it really is the drain business.

Now obviously there's going to be work up front in the Admin of setting up your account, finding the right product and getting it from your supplier to Amazon. There is, of course, going to be admin work, but as you can see there's amazing benefits.

You spend a lot of your life skiing and with your horse and stuff, so the benefits are well worth it.

Sophie Howard: I'm the only mom that picks up her kids from school. We were in the capital city doing the nine to five grind and commuting and all the costs that go with that lifestyle, and now were in a more rural place, which is what we wanted lifestyle wise.

The kid's ski as part of their school, and we ski and we just live in a beautiful place in the South Island of New Zealand. And so, we are really living the dream and it's been possible because of the Amazon income.

Interviewer: So why do you share your Amazon info with others. It's so valuable!

Sophie Howard: Well, firstly I really love helping people do this. And secondly, there are way more profitable products out there than I could ever hope to launch myself. So, I have nothing to lose by helping others do it and everything to gain because I love seeing people get really good results and do a lot of the teaching face to face or in person or live, which really gives me a lot of energy back and I love helping see people get results. And it's been really fun doing this whole Amazon thing start to finish. Just the products, the people involved, being able to help other entrepreneurs pick the right model and pick the right products to sell online.

If getting started as an Amazon seller sounds like the right thing for you now, then what you should do is click on the link, and you'll be able to find out more exactly about what it takes to get started and get your own first Amazon product up and selling.

And you can just be one product away from that income stream, six or seven figures potentially, through selling profitable products on Amazon. So look forward to seeing you, and all the very best. Hope you make it as a successful Amazon seller.*

---

*   Results in interview not typical for illustrative purposes only.

Exercise 2:

List 5 ways your life could change if you had money each month coming in from an Amazon business:

1. _____

2. _____

3. _____

4. _____

5. _____

FAST-START ONLINE MASTERCLASS

HOT SELLING AMAZON PRODUCTS
AND HOW TO FIND THEM

CLICK HERE TO REGISTER NOW

CHAPTER FIVE

100 HOT AMAZON PRODUCTS

100 Hot Selling Amazon Products

It's really inspiring to see how the sales results of everyday products on Amazon.

So, to give you a bit of a head-start, here's a list of 100 hot selling products on Amazon - with an indication/estimation of how much they are selling per month, based on our product analysis process.

Now these results are not typical – most products people launch won't be this popular. But, hopefully they can show you what's possible when you really find a big winner product to sell on Amazon.

ART, SEWING AND CRAFTS*

Tape Measure for Sewing and Tailoring Fabric (Retractable Dual Sided)

EST. SALES
$46,487
PER MONTH

https://www.amazon.com/Measure-Measuring-Sewing-Measurements-Retractable/dp/B071XGLB1S

12 Pairs Tassel Earrings Bohemian Jewelry for Women and Girls - Party Gifts

EST. SALES
$26,706
PER MONTH

https://www.amazon.com/Outee-Earrings-Bohemian-Valentine-Birthday/dp/B07QKDSYYV

* Please note all sales figures are indicative only and subject to change. Extensive independent due diligence should be taken before launching a product on Amazon.

Luna Bean LARGE KEEPSAKE HANDS CASTING KIT | DIY Plaster Statue Molding Kit for COUPLES, Adult & Child, Wedding, Anniversary | 50% More Mold Making Materials and Larger Bucket

EST. SALES
$132,090
PER MONTH

https://www.amazon.com/Luna-Bean-KEEPSAKE-Plaster-Materials/dp/B01E4LWBLQ

Novelinks Photo Case 4" x 6" Photo Box Storage - 16 Inner Photo Keeper Photo Organizer Cases

EST. SALES
$31,760
PER MONTH

https://www.amazon.com/Novelinks-Photo-Case-Storage-Multi-Colored/dp/B07N7N5SMR

Clear Casting and Coating Epoxy Resin - 16 Ounce Kit

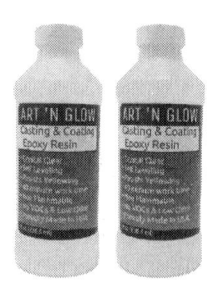

EST. SALES
$157,200
PER MONTH

https://www.amazon.com/Novelinks-Photo-Case-Storage-Multi-Colored/dp/B07N7N5SMR

Tulip X-Large Block Party Tie Dye Kit 16oz

EST. SALES
$65,039
PER MONTH

https://www.amazon.com/Novelinks-Photo-Case-Storage-Multi-Colored/dp/B07N7N5SMR

Face Paint Kit for Kids - 60 Jumbo Stencils, 15 Large Water Based Paints, 2 Glitters - Halloween Makeup Kit, Professional Face Paint Palette, Face Paints Safe for Sensitive Skin, Face Painting Book

EST. SALES
$49,035
PER MONTH

https://www.amazon.com/Novelinks-Photo-Case-Storage-Multi-Colored/dp/B07N7N5SMR

T-Sign 66" Reinforced Artist Easel Stand, Extra Thick Aluminum Metal Tripod Display Easel 21" to 66" Adjustable Height with Portable Bag for Floor/Table-Top Drawing and Displaying

EST. SALES
$64,668
PER MONTH

https://www.amazon.com/Reinforced-Aluminum-Adjustable-Table-Top-Displaying/dp/B076X3WZHB

11 X 14 Inch Stretched Canvas Value Pack of 7

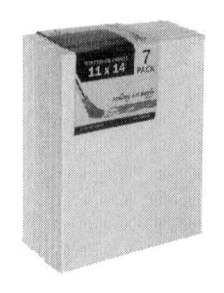

EST. SALES
$48,780
PER MONTH

https://www.amazon.com/Reinforced-Aluminum-Adjustable-Table-Top-Displaying/ dp/B076X3WZHB

Acrylic Paint Pens for Rocks Painting, Ceramic, Glass, Wood, Fabric, Canvas, Mugs, DIY Craft Making Supplies, Scrapbooking Craft, Card Making. Acrylic Paint Marker Pens Permanent.12 Colors/Set

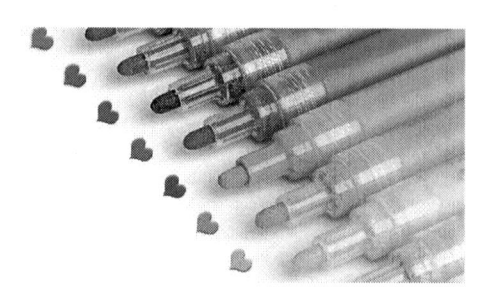

EST. SALES
$42,096
PER MONTH

https://www.amazon.com/Acrylic-Painting-Ceramic-Suppliesg-Permanent/ dp/ B07DB1TVND

AMAZON BOOM 2020

BEAUTY AND PERSONAL CARE*

WOW Apple Cider Vinegar Shampoo & Hair Conditioner Set - (2 x 16.9 Fl Oz / 500mL)

EST. SALES
$369,190
PER MONTH

https://www.amazon.com/Apple-Cider-Vinegar-Shampoo-Conditioner/dp/B07HRNLW6V

TruSkin Vitamin C Serum for Face, Topical Facial Serum with Hyaluronic Acid, Vitamin E, 1oz

EST. SALES
$244,118
PER MONTH

https://www.amazon.com/TruSkin-Naturals-Vitamin-Topical-Hyaluronic/dp/B01M4MCUAF

---

* Please note all sales figures are indicative only and subject to change. Extensive independent due diligence should be taken before launching a product on Amazon.

TheraBreath Fresh Breath Oral Rinse, Mild Mint, 16 Ounce Bottle (Pack of 2)

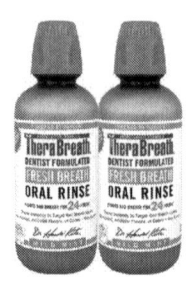

EST. SALES
$132,947
PER MONTH

https://www.amazon.com/TheraBreath-Formulated-Artificial-Certified-Two-Pack/dp/B001ET76AI

Chloven 45 Pcs Hair Scrunchies Velvet Elastics, Bobbles, Hair Bands, Scrunchy Hair Ties

EST. SALES
$77,582
PER MONTH

https://www.amazon.com/Chloven-Scrunchies-Elastics-Scrunchie-Accessories/dp/B07KC2TH9Z

BEAKEY 5 Pcs Makeup Sponge Set Blender Beauty Foundation Blending Sponge, Flawless for Liquid, Cream, and Powder, Multi-colored Makeup Sponges

EST. SALES
$109,930
PER MONTH

https://www.amazon.com/BEAKEY-Foundation-Blending-Flawless-Multi-colored/dp/B01F36JEXE

Propidren by HairGenics - DHT Blocker & Hair Growth Supplement with Saw Palmetto & Biotin - Prevent Hair Loss and Stimulate growth

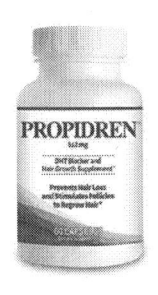

EST. SALES
$251,817
PER MONTH

https://www.amazon.com/Propidren-HairGenics-Palmetto-Stimulate-Follicles/dp/B01NBH0C91

Batiste Dry Shampoo, Original Fragrance, 6.73 Fl Oz, Pack of 3

EST. SALES
$132,937
PER MONTH

https://www.amazon.com/Batiste-Shampoo-Original-Fragrance-Count/dp/B01CYDXMSW

Bath Pillow By Soothing Company | Bathtub Cushion for Neck, Head, Shoulder and Back Support | Jacuzzi Hot Tub Headrest and Bath Tub Pillow.

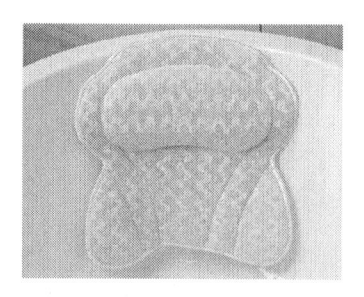

EST. SALES
$53,327
PER MONTH

https://www.amazon.com/Soothing-Company-Bathtub-Shoulders-Luxurious/dp/B07BFRGXZH

24 Organic & Natural Bath Bombs, Handmade Bubble Bath Bomb Gift Set, Rich in Essential Oil, Shea Butter, Coconut Oil, Grape Seed Oil

EST. SALES
$95,970
PER MONTH

https://www.amazon.com/Organic-Natural-Handmade-Essential-Moisturize/dp/B07BFB1YFC

Dry Skin Body Brush - Improves Skin's Health and Beauty - Natural Bristle

EST. SALES
$81,879
PER MONTH

https://www.amazon.com/Dry-Skin-Body-Brush-Circulation/dp/B00LIBEBTG

INDUSTRIAL AND SCIENTIFIC*

Crystal Clear Bar Table Top Epoxy Resin Coating for Wood Tabletop - 1 Gallon Kit

EST. SALES
$404,960
PER MONTH

https://www.amazon.com/Crystal-Clear-Table-Coating-Tabletop/dp/B01LYK-2NAG

Medline Heavy Absorbency 36" x 36" Quilted Fluff and Polymer Disposable Underpads, 50 Per Case, Great Protection for Beds, Furniture, Surfaces

EST. SALES
$291,724
PER MONTH

https://www.amazon.com/Medline-Absorbency-Disposable-Underpads-Protection/dp/B002NHIFNW

*   Please note all sales figures are indicative only and subject to change. Extensive independent due diligence should be taken before launching a product on Amazon.

AMMEX Nitrile Disposable Gloves - Powder-Free, Latex-Free, Food Safe, Industrial, 5 mil, Large, Black (Box of 100)

EST. SALES
$110,733
PER MONTH

https://www.amazon.com/AMMEX-GPNB46100-BX-GlovePlus-Disposable-Industrial/dp/B004BR8KB4

Catchmaster 904 Bug & Fly Clear Window Fly Traps - 3 Packs of 4 Traps

EST. SALES
$291,724
PER MONTH

https://www.amazon.com/Catchmaster-904-Clear-Window-Traps/dp/B001QBPP66

Chapin International 617407731200 Chapin 20002 2-Gallon Poly Lawn, Garden, and Multi-Purpose Or Home Pro, 2 gal, Translucent White

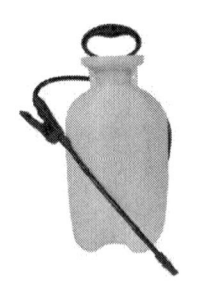

EST. SALES
$130,714
PER MONTH

https://www.amazon.com/Chapin-International-617407731200-20002-Multi-Purpose/dp/B0039EEN0M

Biofreeze Pain Relief Gel for Arthritis, 3 oz. Roll-on Topical Analgesic, Fast Acting and Long Lasting Cooling Pain Reliever Cream for Muscle Pain, Joint Pain

EST. SALES
$53,903
PER MONTH

https://www.amazon.com/Biofreeze-Arthritis-Analgesic-Reliever-Colorless/dp/ B0056PRKJI

DIYMAG Powerful Neodymium Disc Magnets, Strong, Permanent, Rare Earth Magnets. Fridge, DIY, Building, Scientific, Craft, and Office Magnets, 1.26"D x 1/8"H, Pack of 6

EST. SALES
$24,940
PER MONTH

https://www.amazon.com/DIYMAG-Powerful-Neodymium-Permanent-Scientific/dp/B06XD2X45M

Superfeet GREEN Insoles, Professional-Grade High Arch Orthotic Insert for Maximum Support, Unisex, Green

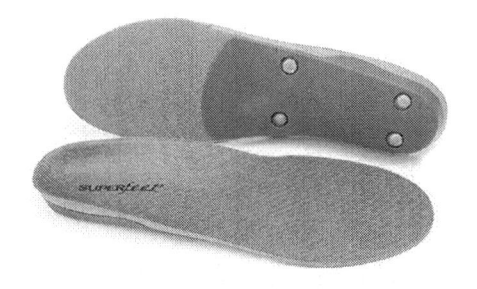

EST. SALES
$411,573
PER MONTH

https://www.amazon.com/Superfeet-GREEN-Length-Insole-Green/dp/B001CD9ULY

Night Wrist Sleep Support Brace - Fits Both Hands - Cushioned to Help with Carpal Tunnel and Relieve and Treat Wrist Pain, Adjustable, Fitted-ComfyBrace

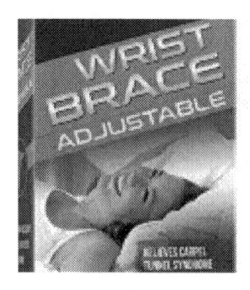

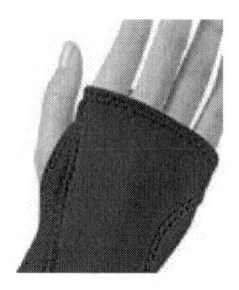

EST. SALES
$120,942
PER MONTH

https://www.amazon.com/Night-Wrist-Sleep-Support-Brace/dp/B074MKSSHK

BLITZU Plantar Fasciitis Socks with Arch Support, Foot Care Compression Sleeve, Eases Swelling & Heel Spurs, Ankle Brace Support, Relieve Pain Fast

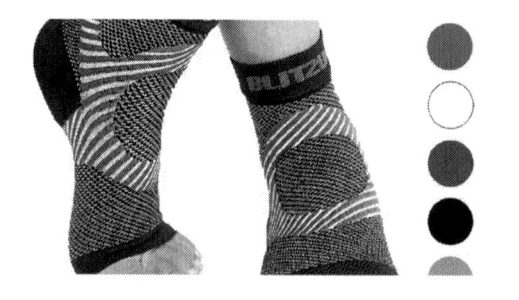

EST. SALES
$51,347
PER MONTH

https://www.amazon.com/BLITZU-Plantar-Fasciitis-Compression-Swelling/dp/B01ETP3VAM

AMAZON BOOM 2020

PATIO LAWN AND GARDEN*

Keter Novel Plastic Deck Storage Container Box Outdoor Patio Furniture 90 Gal, Brown

EST. SALES
$375,582
PER MONTH

$68.99
PER ITEM

https://www.amazon.com/Keter-Plastic-Storage-Container-Furniture/dp/B00JXRFFJM

Orbit 58910 Programmable Hose Faucet Timer, 2 Outlet, Green

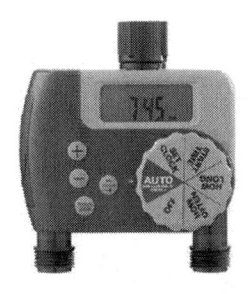

EST. SALES
$713.097
PER MONTH

$44.07
PER ITEM

https://www.amazon.com/Orbit-58910-2-Outlet-Programmable-Faucet/dp/B008VDULGG

---

* Please note all sales figures are indicative only and subject to change. Extensive independent due diligence should be taken before launching a product on Amazon.

Flowtron BK-40D Electronic Insect Killer, 1 Acre Coverage

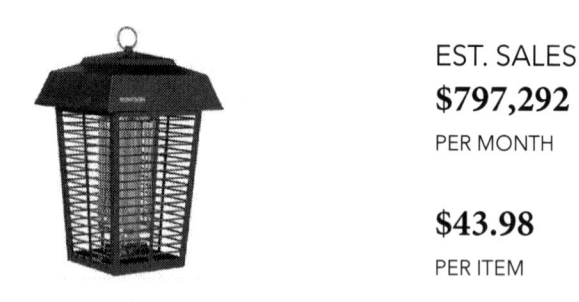

EST. SALES
$797,292
PER MONTH

$43.98
PER ITEM

https://www.amazon.com/Flowtron-BK-40D-Electronic-Insect-Coverage/dp/B00004R9VW

Sunnyglade 9' Patio Umbrella Outdoor Table Umbrella with 8 Sturdy Ribs (Beige)

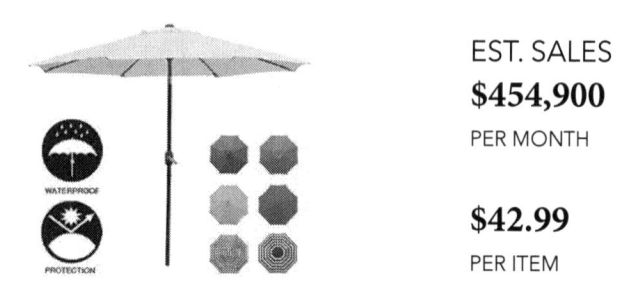

EST. SALES
$454,900
PER MONTH

$42.99
PER ITEM

https://www.amazon.com/Sunnyglade-Patio-Umbrella-Outdoor-Sturdy/dp/B07KXLQHF2

DC America UBP18181-BR 18-Inch Cast Stone Umbrella Base, Made from Rust Free Composite Materials, Bronze Powder Coated Finish

EST. SALES
$327,140
PER MONTH

$29.74
PER ITEM

https://www.amazon.com/America-UBP18181-BR-Umbrella-Composite-Materials/dp/B0025VP5J8

VicTsing Grill Cover, Small 30-Inch Waterproof, Heavy Duty Gas Grill Cover

EST. SALES
$230,842
PER MONTH

$18.99
PER ITEM

https://www.amazon.com/VicTsing-30-Inch-Waterproof-Brinkmann-Holland/dp/B01MRQVYKC

GRILLART Grill Brush and Scraper Best BBQ Brush for Grill, Safe 18" Stainless Steel Woven Wire 3 in 1 Bristles Grill Cleaning Brush for Weber Gas/Charcoal Grill, Gifts for Grill Wizard Grate Cleaner

EST. SALES
$203,725
PER MONTH

$16.97
PER ITEM

https://www.amazon.com/GRILLART-Grill-Brush-Stainless-Bristles/dp/B075NC2MYB

Intex Solar Cover for 10ft Diameter Easy Set and Frame Pools

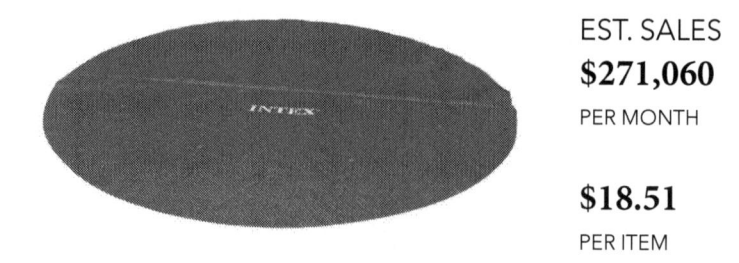

EST. SALES
$271,060
PER MONTH

$18.51
PER ITEM

https://www.amazon.com/Intex-Solar-Cover-Diameter-Frame/dp/B00P7O-4KAU

12 Pack Mosquito Repellent Bracelet Band - [320Hrs] of Premium Pest Control Insect Bug Repeller - Natural Indoor/Outdoor Insects

EST. SALES
$141,910
PER MONTH

$14.99
PER ITEM

https://www.amazon.com/Pack-Mosquito-Repellent-Bracelet-Band/dp/B07NNZFYLZ

Keter 7.5-Gal Cool Bar Rattan Style Outdoor Patio Pool Cooler Table, Brown

EST. SALES
$491,498
PER MONTH

$59.99
PER ITEM

https://www.amazon.com/Keter-7-5-Gal-Rattan-Outdoor-Cooler/dp/B007O-1CAZQ

Elucto Large Electric Bug Zapper Fly Swatter Zap Mosquito Best for Indoor and Outdoor Pest Control (2 DURACELL AA Batteries Included)

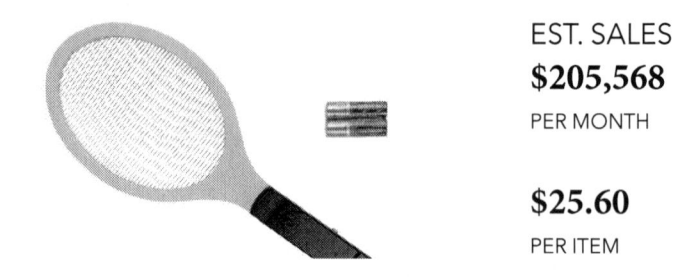

EST. SALES
$205,568
PER MONTH

$25.60
PER ITEM

https://www.amazon.com/Elucto-Electric-Mosquito-DURACELL-Batteries/dp/B073PXV2GW

Vivere C9POLY-13 Hammock, Aqua

EST. SALES
$1,190,693
PER MONTH

$123.58
PER ITEM

https://www.amazon.com/Vivere-C9POLY-13-Hammock-Aqua/dp/B07L3LSL-HB

AMAZON BOOM 2020

TOYS AND GAMES*

Step2 Rain Showers Splash Pond Water Table | Kids Water Play Table with 13-Pc Accessory Set

EST. SALES
$332,587
PER MONTH

$62.99
PER ITEM

https://www.amazon.com/Step2-874600-Showers-Playset-Multi-Colored/dp/B01K1K0K6M

SwimWays Baby Spring Float Activity Center with Canopy - Inflatable Float for Children with Interactive Toys and UPF Sun Protection - Blue/Green Octopus

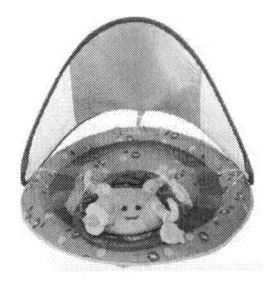

EST. SALES
$203,936
PER MONTH

$29.75
PER ITEM

* Please note all sales figures are indicative only and subject to change. Extensive independent due diligence should be taken before launching a product on Amazon.

https://www.amazon.com/SwimWays-Spring-Activity-Center-Octopus/dp/B000WQZD9U

Click N' Play Pack of 200 Phthalate Free BPA Free Crush Proof Plastic Ball, Pit Balls - 6 Bright Colors in Reusable and Durable Storage Mesh Bag with Zipper

EST. SALES
$136,344
PER MONTH

$26.49
PER ITEM

https://www.amazon.com/Click-Play-Phthalate-Crush-Plastic/dp/B00PYLU3GG

Made By Me Create Your Own Window Art by Horizon Group USA, Paint Your Own Suncatchers, Includes 12 Suncatchers & More, Assorted Colors

EST. SALES
$49,700
PER MONTH

$9.97
PER ITEM

https://www.amazon.com/Made-Me-Create-Window-Assorted/dp/B00HUBBDIK

SplashEZ 3-in-1 Sprinkler for Kids, Splash Pad, and Wading Pool for Learning Children's Sprinkler Pool, 60" Inflatable Water Toys – "from A to Z" Outdoor Swimming Pool for Babies and Toddlers

EST. SALES
$153,033
PER MONTH

$26.99
PER ITEM

https://www.amazon.com/SplashEZ-Sprinkler-Splash-Wading-Learning/dp/B07MNMT3M7

Intex Rainbow Ring Inflatable Play Center, 117" X 76" X 53", for Ages 2+

EST. SALES
$275,099
PER MONTH

$47.39
PER ITEM

https://www.amazon.com/Intex-Rainbow-Ring-Inflatable-Center/dp/B000KI111Y

SKLZ Pro Mini Basketball Hoop with Ball, Standard (18 x 12 inches)

EST. SALES
$115,454
PER MONTH

$24.99
PER ITEM

https://www.amazon.com/SKLZ-Basketball-Shatter-Resistant-Backboard/dp/B001I912SQ

Stomp Rocket Dueling Rockets, 4 Rockets and Rocket Launcher - Outdoor Rocket Toy Gift for Boys and Girls Ages 6 Years and Up

EST. SALES
$57,708
PER MONTH

$19.99
PER ITEM

https://www.amazon.com/Stomp-Rocket-Dueling-Rockets-Packaging/dp/B00GAC6470

Sunny Days Entertainment Maxx Bubbles Bubble-N-Go Toy Mower with Refill Solution

EST. SALES
$80,040
PER MONTH

$16.99
PER ITEM

https://www.amazon.com/Bubbles-Bubble-N-Go-Mower-Refill-Solution/dp/B00V5BNSIE

WOWMAZING Giant Bubble Wands Kit: (3-Piece Set) | Incl. Wand, Big Bubble Concentrate and Tips & Trick Booklet | Outdoor Toy for Kids, Boys, Girls | Bubbles Made in The USA (Kit)

EST. SALES
$62,267
PER MONTH

$14.95
PER ITEM

https://www.amazon.com/WOWmazing-Giant-Bubble-Wands-Kit/dp/B01CK78BLA

SOPHIE HOWARD

TOOLS AND HOME IMPROVEMENT

AquaBliss High Output 12-Stage Shower Filter - Reduces Dry Itchy Skin, Dandruff, Eczema, and Dramatically Improves The Condition of Your Skin, Hair and Nails - Chrome (SF100)

EST. SALES

$178,483

PER MONTH

$34.86

PER ITEM

https://www.amazon.com/AquaBliss-Output-12-Stage-Shower-Filter/dp/B01MUBU0YC

Smart plug, Gosund Mini Wifi Outlet Works With Alexa, Google Home & IFTTT, No Hub Required, Remote Control Your Home Appliances from Anywhere, ETL Certified,Only Supports 2.4GHz Network(4 Pieces)

EST. SALES

$166,764

PER MONTH

$32.99

PER ITEM

https://www.amazon.com/Gosund-Compatible-Required-appliances-Certified/dp/B079MFTYMV

AquaDance High Pressure 6-Setting 3.5" Chrome Face Handheld Shower with Hose for the Ultimate Shower Experience! Officially Independently Tested to Meet Strict US Quality & Performance Standards!

EST. SALES
$89,588
PER MONTH

$16.99
PER ITEM

https://www.amazon.com/AquaDance-Experience-Officially-Independently-Performance/dp/B01H2DG1SW

UV Flashlight Black light UV Lights , Vansky 51 LED Ultraviolet Blacklight Pet Urine Detector For Dog/Cat Urine,Dry Stains,Bed Bug, Matching with Pet Odor Eliminator

EST. SALES
$70,432
PER MONTH

$12.99
PER ITEM

https://www.amazon.com/Flashlight-Vansky-Ultraviolet-Blacklight-Eliminator/dp/B01A5KLUG2

Intex 28003E Deluxe Pool Maintenance Kit for Above Ground Pools

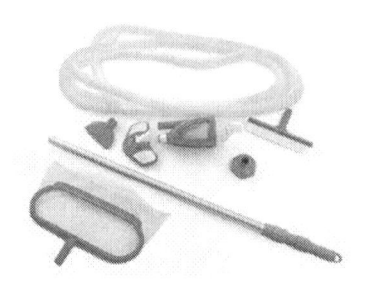

EST. SALES
$167,637
PER MONTH

$32.98
PER ITEM

https://www.amazon.com/Intex-Deluxe-Maintenance-Above-Ground/dp/B005QIXOY0

Flux Phenom Reinforced Magnetic Screen Door, Fits Doors Up to 38 x 82-Inch

EST. SALES
$188,175
PER MONTH

$28.95
PER ITEM

https://www.amazon.com/Flux-Phenom-Reinforced-Magnetic-82-Inch/dp/B01ESSA9VO

AMAZON BOOM 2020

Master Lock 5400D Set Your Own Combination Portable Lock Box, 5 Key Capacity, Black

EST. SALES
$97,726
PER MONTH

$16.99
PER ITEM

https://www.amazon.com/Master-Lock-5400D-Combination-Portable/dp/B0002YP1VC

Filtrete 20x25x1, AC Furnace Air Filter, MPR 300, Clean Living Basic Dust, 6-Pack

EST. SALES
$132,598
PER MONTH

$27.48
PER ITEM

https://www.amazon.com/Filtrete-20x25x1-MPR-300-Furnace/dp/B07FNXPGLG

SOPHIE HOWARD

78 LED Closet Light, Newest Version Rechargeable Motion Sensor Closet Light Wireless Under Cabinet Light with Large Battery Life 2400mAh for Closet,Cabinet,Wardrobe,Kitchen,Hallway (2 Sensor Modes)

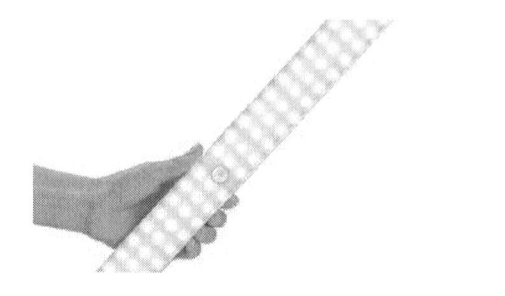

EST. SALES
$61,774
PER MONTH

$23.99
PER ITEM

https://www.amazon.com/Version-Rechargeable-Wireless-Cabinet-Wardrobe/ dp/B07FNXJC8G

Original Blackout Pleated Paper Shade Black, 36" x 72", 6-Pack

EST. SALES
$136,450
PER MONTH

$29.49
PER ITEM

https://www.amazon.com/Original-Blackout-Pleated-Shade-6-Pack/dp/B000SDROMG

Seville Classics 3-Tier Resin Slat Utility Shoe Rack, Espresso

EST. SALES
$98,037
PER MONTH

$29.99
PER ITEM

https://www.amazon.com/Seville-Classics-3-Tier-Utility-Espresso/dp/B00336TY0K

SOPHIE HOWARD

SPORTS AND OUTDOOR*

VENUZOR Waist Trainer Belt for Women - Waist Cincher Trimmer - Slimming Body Shaper Belt - Sport Girdle Belt (UP Graded)

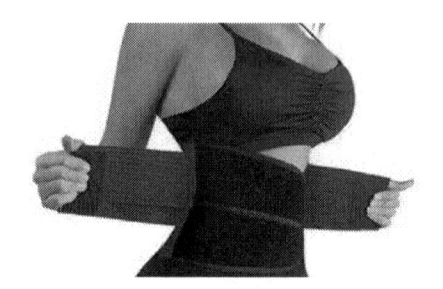

EST. SALES
$123,672
PER MONTH

$13.99
PER ITEM

https://www.amazon.com/VENUZOR-Waist-Trainer-Belt-Women/dp/B07F33VNJY

Sawyer Products Premium Insect Repellent with 20% Picaridin

EST. SALES
$870,640
PER MONTH

$80.00
PER ITEM

https://www.amazon.com/Sawyer-Products-SP567-Repellent-0-5-Gallon/dp/B01M4RCAVO

*   Please note all sales figures are indicative only and subject to change. Extensive independent due diligence should be taken before launching a product on Amazon.

LETSCOM Fitness Tracker HR, Activity Tracker Watch with Heart Rate Monitor, Waterproof Smart Fitness Band with Step Counter, Calorie Counter, Pedometer Watch for Kids Women and Men

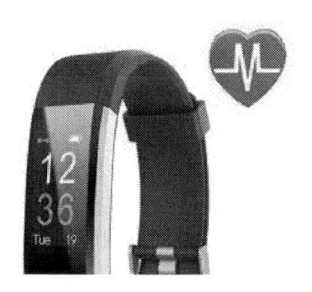

EST. SALES
$235,433
PER MONTH

$29.98
PER ITEM

https://www.amazon.com/LETSCOM-Fitness-Activity-Waterproof-Pedometer/dp/B0779SKCXW

YETI Rambler 20 oz Stainless Steel Vacuum Insulated Tumbler w/MagSlider Lid

EST. SALES
$289,731
PER MONTH

$29.90
PER ITEM

https://www.amazon.com/YETI-Rambler-Stainless-Insulated-MagSlider/dp/B073WJMKHN

Coleman Portable Camping Quad Chair with 4-Can Cooler

EST. SALES
$167,433
PER MONTH

$24.99
PER ITEM

https://www.amazon.com/Coleman-Cooler-Portable-Camping-Chair/dp/B0033990ZQ

Trideer Exercise Ball (45-85cm) Extra Thick Yoga Ball Chair, Anti-Burst Heavy Duty Stability Ball Supports 2200lbs, Birthing Ball with Quick Pump (Office & Home & Gym)

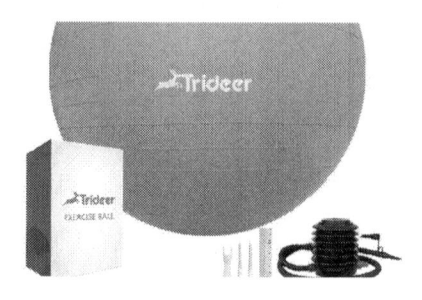

EST. SALES
$128,752
PER MONTH

$18.99
PER ITEM

https://www.amazon.com/Trideer-Exercise-Anti-Burst-Stability-Supports/dp/B07DKHCN3R

Physix Gear Compression Socks for Men & Women (20-30 mmHg) Best Graduated Athletic Fit for Running, Nurses, Shin Splints, Flight Travel & Maternity Pregnancy - Boost Stamina, Circulation & Recovery

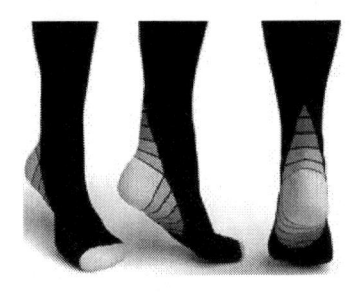

EST. SALES
$146,105
PER MONTH

$18.95
PER ITEM

https://www.amazon.com/Physix-Gear-Compression-Graduated-Maternity/dp/B01J4MF19O

Sport-Brella Versa-Brella SPF 50+ Adjustable Umbrella with Universal Clamp

EST. SALES
$139,674
PER MONTH

$17.99
PER ITEM

https://www.amazon.com/Sport-Brella-Versa-Brella-Swiveling-Umbrella-Firebrick/dp/B00HA2ZKFQ

BalanceFrom GoYoga All-Purpose 1/2-Inch Extra Thick High Density Anti-Tear Exercise Yoga Mat with Carrying Strap

EST. SALES
$116,455
PER MONTH

$15.99
PER ITEM

https://www.amazon.com/BalanceFrom-BFGY-AP6BLK-Anti-Tear-Exercise-Carrying/dp/B00FO9U46W

Natural Shoe Deodorizer Spray, Foot Odor Eliminator and Air Freshener - Organic Lemongrass, Mint, Tea Tree Essential Oils

EST. SALES
$74,139
PER MONTH

$12.95
PER ITEM

https://www.amazon.com/Lumi-Outdoors-Deodorizer-Eliminator-Freshener/dp/B013TSRYUS

AMAZON BOOM 2020

KITCHEN AND DINING*

Dash Mini Maker: The Mini Waffle Maker Machine for Individual Waffles, Paninis, Hash browns, & other on the go Breakfast, Lunch, or Snacks - Aqua

EST. SALES
$145,504
PER MONTH

$9.99
PER ITEM

https://www.amazon.com/Dash-Mini-Maker-Individual-Breakfast/dp/B01M9I779L

Berry Ave Broom Holder and Garden Tool Organizer Rake or Mop Handles Up to 1.25-Inches, Small, Black

EST. SALES
$154,885
PER MONTH

https://www.amazon.com/Berry-Ave-Broom-Holder-1-25-Inches/dp/B01DI8H364

* Please note all sales figures are indicative only and subject to change. Extensive independent due diligence should be taken before launching a product on Amazon.

BrüMate Hopsulator Slim Double-walled Stainless Steel Insulated Can Cooler for 12 Oz Slim Cans (Glitter Violet)

EST. SALES
$352,207
PER MONTH

https://www.amazon.com/BrüMate-Hopsulator-Double-walled-Stainless-Insulated/dp/B07K2KWNFD

Ozeri ZK14-S Pronto Digital Multifunction Kitchen and Food Scale, Elegant Black

EST. SALES
$123,967
PER MONTH

https://www.amazon.com/Ozeri-ZK14-S-Digital-Multifunction-Kitchen/dp/B004164SRA

Lodge LMS3 Miniature Skillet, 3.5", Black

EST. SALES
$71,122
PER MONTH

https://www.amazon.com/Lodge-Skillet-Miniature-Individual-Desserts/dp/B000LXA9YI

ThermoPro TP03 Digital Instant Read Meat Thermometer Kitchen Cooking Food Candy Thermometer for Oil Deep Fry BBQ Grill Smoker Thermometer

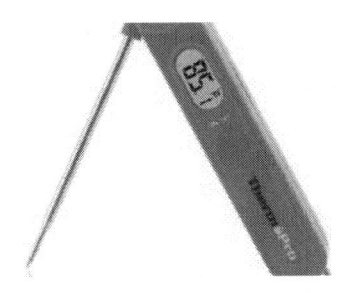

EST. SALES
$175,417
PER MONTH

https://www.amazon.com/ThermoPro-TP03A-Digital-Instant-Thermometer/dp/B01IHHLB3W

Stasher Pocket 100% Silicone Bags, Small Storage Size, 4.5"/4oz), Clear + Aqua

EST. SALES
$175,015
PER MONTH

https://www.amazon.com/Stasher-Pocket-Silicone-Small-Storage/dp/B07RC84B75

Fit & Fresh Cool Coolers Slim Ice Packs for Coolers/ Lunch Bags/Lunch Boxes/ Office/Jobsite/Camping/ Beach/Picnics/Golfing, for All Ages, Set of 4, Blue

EST. SALES
$98,549
PER MONTH

https://www.amazon.com/Fit-Fresh-Coolers-Reusable-Packs/dp/B003FO-2B5U

GuGio Lunch Bag Insulated Lunch Box Reusable Lunch Tote Cooler Organizer Bag Lunch Bags for Women Ladies Adults

EST. SALES
$25,079
PER MONTH

https://www.amazon.com/Insulated-Reusable-Cooler-Organizer-Ladies/dp/B07SPG2HC2

Aqua 1 Pack Premium Disposable Plastic Tablecloth 54 Inch. x 108 Inch. Rectangle Table Cover By Dluxware

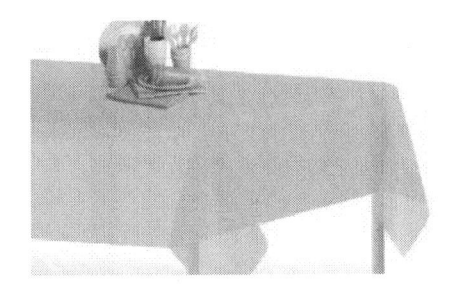

EST. SALES
$74,080
PER MONTH

https://www.amazon.com/Premium-Disposable-Tablecloth-Rectangle-Dluxware/dp/B078X2LVK2

SOPHIE HOWARD

GROCERY AND GOURMET

HighKey Snacks Keto Mini Cookies – Chocolate Chip, Pack of 3, 2.25oz Bags Keto Friendly, Gluten Free, Low Carb, Healthy Snack - Sweet, Diet Friendly Dessert

EST. SALES
$348,775
PER MONTH

https://www.amazon.com/HighKey-Snacks-Keto-Mini-Cookies/dp/B07JYS-45BT

Viva Naturals Organic Extra Virgin Coconut Oil, 16 Ounce

EST. SALES
$204,573
PER MONTH

https://www.amazon.com/Viva-Naturals-Organic-Virgin-Coconut/dp/B00D-S842HS

AMAZON BOOM 2020

BetterBody Foods Organic Chia Seeds with Omega-3, Non-GMO (2 lbs.)

EST. SALES
$103,187
PER MONTH

https://www.amazon.com/BetterBody-Foods-Contains-Gluten-free-Smoothies/dp/B00MPQ5ZOS

Spectrum Essentials Organic Ground Flaxseed, 24 oz

EST. SALES
$138,709
PER MONTH

https://www.amazon.com/Spectrum-Essentials-Organic-Ground-Flaxseed/dp/B00DOKFLYI

ChocZero's Keto Bark, Dark Chocolate Almonds with Sea Salt. Sugar Free, Low Carb. No Sugar Alcohols, No Artificial Sweeteners, All Natural, Non-GMO (2 bags, 6 servings/each)

EST. SALES
$261,486
PER MONTH

https://www.amazon.com/ChocZeros-Chocolate-Stone-Ground-Artificial-Sweeteners/dp/B0799CH1ZZ

PBfit All-Natural Peanut Butter Powder, Powdered Peanut Spread from Real Roasted Pressed Peanuts, 8g of Protein (30 oz.)

EST. SALES
$173,802
PER MONTH

https://www.amazon.com/PBfit-All-Natural-Roasted-Pressed-Ingredients/dp/B01KKEECLS

Lakanto Monkfruit 1: 1 Sugar Substitute | 3 lb NON GMO (Classic White)

EST. SALES
$369,012
PER MONTH

https://www.amazon.com/Lakanto-Monkfruit-Sugar-Substitute-Classic/dp/B01LDNBAC4

Bai Flavored Water, Rainforest Variety Pack, Antioxidant Infused Drinks, 18 Fluid Ounce Bottles, 12 count, 3 each of Brasilia Blueberry, Costa Rica Clementine, Malawi Mango, Sumatra Dragonfruit

EST. SALES
$192,983
PER MONTH

https://www.amazon.com/Rainforest-Antioxidant-Blueberry-Clementine-Dragonfruit/dp/B0088MXS6U

Jade Leaf Matcha Green Tea Powder - USDA Organic, Authentic Japanese Origin - Classic Culinary Grade (Smoothies, Lattes, Baking, Recipes) - Antioxidants, Energy [30g Starter Size]

EST. SALES
$135,907
PER MONTH

https://www.amazon.com/Jade-Leaf-Matcha-Green-Powder/dp/B00PF-DH0IC

Fat Snax Cookies - Low Carb, Keto, and Sugar Free (Variety Pack, 6-pack (12 cookies)) - Keto-Friendly & Gluten-Free Snack Foods

EST. SALES
$75,191
PER MONTH

https://www.amazon.com/Fat-Snax-Cookies-Variety-cookies/dp/B074WCZ-6RL

AMAZON BOOM 2020

HEALTH AND HOUSEHOLD*

Collagen Peptides Powder (16oz) | Grass-Fed, Certified Paleo Friendly, Non-Gmo and Gluten Free - Unflavored

EST. SALES
$769,324
PER MONTH

https://www.amazon.com/Collagen-Peptides-Grass-Fed-Certified-Friendly/dp/B00XQ2XGAA

Turmeric Curcumin with Bioperine 1500mg. Highest Potency Available. Premium Pain Relief & Joint Support with 95% Standardized Curcuminoids. Non-GMO, Gluten Free Turmeric...

EST. SALES
$440,577
PER MONTH

---

*   Please note all sales figures are indicative only and subject to change. Extensive independent due diligence should be taken before launching a product on Amazon.

https://www.amazon.com/Turmeric-Bioperine-Available-Standardized-Curcuminoids/dp/B01DBTFO98

Prime Labs - Men's Test Booster - Natural Stamina, Endurance and Strength Booster - 60 Caplets

EST. SALES
$368,895
PER MONTH

https://www.amazon.com/Prime-Labs-Testosterone-Booster-Caplets/dp/B01MQ1JLWY

Cali White ACTIVATED CHARCOAL & ORGANIC COCONUT OIL TEETH WHITENING TOOTHPASTE, MADE IN USA, Best Natural Whitener, Vegan, Fluoride Free, Sulfate Free, Organic,

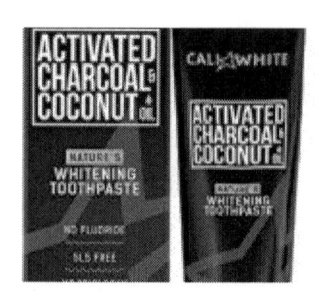

EST. SALES
$202,547
PER MONTH

https://www.amazon.com/Cali-White-ACTIVATED-WHITENING-TOOTHPASTE/dp/B06WRS71N8

Dr Tobias Colon 14 Day Quick Cleanse - Supports Detox & Increased Energy Levels (28 Capsules)

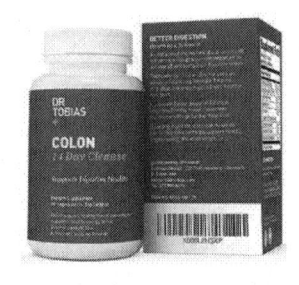

EST. SALES
$223,385
PER MONTH

https://www.amazon.com/Dr-Tobias-Colon-Cleanse-Increased/dp/B00ISAPPLI

Poo-Pourri Before-You-Go Toilet Spray 1 oz Bottle, Original Citrus Scent

EST. SALES
$322,350
PER MONTH

https://www.amazon.com/Poo-Pourri-Before-You-Go-Toilet-Bottle-Original/dp/B07FSYJTDB

Rocco & Roxie Professional Strength Stain & Odor Eliminator - Enzyme-Powered Pet Odor & Stain Remover for Dog and Cats Urine

EST. SALES
$464,362
PER MONTH

https://www.amazon.com/Rocco-Roxie-Supply-Co-Professional/dp/B00CKFL93K

Mr Clean Magic Eraser Extra Durable, Cleaning Pads with Durafoam, 8 Count Box (Packaging May Vary)

EST. SALES
$138,431
PER MONTH

https://www.amazon.com/Clean-Durable-Cleaning-Durafoam-Packaging/dp/ B00BR1FSU8

AMAZON BOOM 2020

Telescopic Reusable Straw, Composed of scurry Collapsible Reusable Stainless Steel Straw and Food-Grade Silicone, Portable Set with Hard Case Holder, for Party, Travel, Household, Outdoor, etc (Pink)

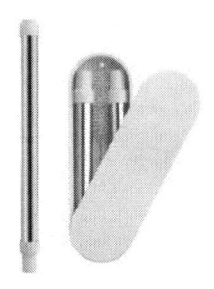

EST. SALES
$164,195
PER MONTH

https://www.amazon.com/dp/B07T96JSHF

Koala Kleaner Alcohol Free Eyeglass Lens Cleaner Spray Care Kit | 16oz + 2 Cloths | Safe for Cleaning All Lenses and Screens

EST. SALES
$89,618
PER MONTH

https://www.amazon.com/Koala-Kleaner-Eyeglass-Microfiber-Cleaning/dp/B0785SB7J6

Exercise 3:

What are 5 products you could sell on Amazon?

(Note: this is just to get you thinking. Obviously before you invest in a product, you will have done moreresearch)

1. _____

2. _____

3. _____

4. _____

5. _____

CHAPTER SIX

QUESTIONS AND ANSWERS WITH THE AMAZON EXPERT SOPHIE HOWARD

I am often approached with questions from people who are interested in selling successfully on Amazon. Here are the questions I am most frequently asked as a professional Amazon seller.

Question 1: Is Amazon still the best place to sell, and is FBA the most effective sales channel?

I've sold over 500 products on Amazon, and I've also sold two of my Amazon businesses, one for over a million US dollars and one for several hundred thousand dollars. So I've launched a lot of products and really figured out what works on this platform and been able to repeat those results as well. So people often ask me, can I still make money with Amazon FBA? And every time I've sold an Amazon business myself, I've asked myself the same question, is this the place to be? Can I still make money here? Well, the short answer is yes. Everything always changes and there's new challenges and it's important to stay up with what strategies are working rather than something that people were teaching that worked five years ago that might not be working.

But if you put the effort into following someone who's getting current results and who's paying attention to what's happening on Amazon and not following the same strategy as everyone else, as soon as you're doing some copycat thing for all the best selling products and the competition's tough, then those margins get thin. But if you have a strategy where you're looking for low competition but high margin products, then yes, you can definitely still make money with Amazon FBA.

I've had all sorts of opportunities to learn about other areas of e-Commerce or business. And I always come back to Amazon because if you can find products that meet certain criteria that give you a healthy profit margin and there's low competition and there are hundreds, if not hundreds of thousands of products like that out there that I can find and I can teach you to find, there's still lots and lots of opportunity on Amazon.

You'll always hear people say, "Oh, it's saturated." But there are naysayers for every single business out there. And I can find products all the time and I can teach other people who want to look and who want to be optimistic and grab an opportunity. I can teach them how to find these profitable products.

There is definitely still plenty of opportunity to make money on Amazon FBA. And the trap for people who say that you can't is that they're following the wrong strategy where they're just finding copycat products from Alibaba and having a price fall on identical products with other sellers who have the same tactics as them. So you need to do it a little bit differently from the mainstream. But when you know the right way to do it, this is the best place to be doing business online, I believe.

Question 2: Is China the best place to source products?

So what's happening with China? This is all the talk at the moment, trade wars and tariffs and what's going on, what's happening with the factories themselves? Are they starting to sell on Amazon directly? And the answer is yes. Where there's huge volumes coming out of non-differentiated, just standard mass produced plastic products straight off the mold, straight off the factory floor and on a container ship over to the US then yes, that is a tough game to be and you don't want to be selling a product on Amazon that's mass produced in China by a factory where you've got no point of difference with your product. You've got no strong branding. That is a tough game.

However, there are still plenty of really good quality products in China. It's not the main country that I've done most of my sourcing from, but certainly I've had some really great profitable, successful products from there. Many of my students who I teach find great products there. Six and seven figure businesses with products coming out of China today.

So the game's changed a little bit. You need to know your numbers when you pick the product. Something that might've looked viable a year ago might now just be borderline or marginal because of some new expenses, and it makes it really important to choose the right kind of product.

Five years ago, you could throw a product up there and hope for the best source from China, sell on Amazon in the US, and you could get away with a bit of beginner's luck. Now that the market's more mature.

You need to actually have a really clear product strategy. So it means that something like a garlic crusher or some silicone spatula set or something really obvious from China is not going to be a winning product on Amazon today. But there are still products where China is the best country to source that product from. And it's also good to get some quotes from Vietnam or India.

There might be other parts of the world that don't have tariffs or have different manufacturing costs. India and Vietnam are a lot cheaper manufacturing than China, and the shipping's pretty much the same.

So I've always looked to diversify and all parts of my business, including which countries I source from. But China's interesting. They're looking to start selling themselves, but they can never write a great listing if English isn't their mother tongue.

They don't get the branding quite right for the west often. So they've got big product capability but they haven't got the marketing. And this game is won on how you present your product and outdo your competition. So somebody who's just got a mas- produced product out of China is not on a winning strategy, but you can learn a winning strategy that doesn't rely on mass-produced products straight off a factory floor in China.

You need to have a point of difference and you need to choose the right kind of product that's low competition and isn't going to attract any copycats or things like that.

And also when you work with your suppliers, if you do that in the right way, they'll become your allies, not a threat to your business. They'll be feeding you product ideas. I got invited to my Chinese suppliers wedding, and they feed me product ideas. They come up with new packaging ideas. They really, really look after me because we have a good relationship.

So when you do business in Asia, you really need to not just learn about what products are going to be profitable on Amazon. You need to learn how to work with your international supply chain.

Youneed to do business with a new cultural understanding and build a relationship with a new person in the business that you're probably not going to get to meet in person, at least in the short term.

Question 3: How do I source from other countries?

That's something I can help you with if you want to learn. And certainly as things change in China, I'm watching it really carefully, but I'm still happy to do business there. The new tariffs are just a new expense, but they apply exactly the same to everyone. And sometimes it's the best place to source from. They've got decades of experience manufacturing and exporting.

They're very professional. They're very fast. The shipping's cheap and they can really scale up with you. So if you're thinking about selling on Amazon, make sure you don't go in blind, make sure you're getting some good advice around exactly how to play the China game.

There are so many places to source from. I've always had some wonderful products selling out of Asia, and I also sourced from Australia, New Zealand where I live, and I also source from within the United States.

Every product is totally different, and part of your product research is figuring out the best place to make that product. So there are some basic questions to ask. There's some online research to do. It is all free. None of it's hard when you know what to ask and where to look, but you do need to really make sure that the raw materials are coming from a place that's quality and cost effective.

The skills of the people making the product or the factories are giving you a price advantage or a quality advantage and that the supply chains can keep up with demands.

I've really enjoyed doing business in India and Vietnam over the last few years. My first product was from Nepal. My second brand was from Sri Lanka. So I've done business all around the world and I don't really have a favorite. It really comes down to which is the best place to source each product.

Question 4: How can I find great manufacturers and suppliers?

I do have a particular fondness for trade shows though because at a trade show you can meet a lot of suppliers in one hit and also see the quality of the product, see new product ideas that you never knew existed until you saw them and really get to build a relationship with the supplier and negotiate face to face, which I think gets you a better result. So that's how I do my sourcing all online.

But the trade show's always fun but not essential, very productive way to get lots of new product ideas. But really with the way suppliers are all online now, the world is at our fingertips, these suppliers are looking to do business and they're keen to hear from us.

If you turn up sounding professional with the right set of questions, then they will want to help you grow your business. So I've always enjoyed working with my suppliers and found some wonderful products by looking all around the world for new things to launch and sell on Amazon.

Question 5: What strategy of product selection works best?

So I could talk about strategy of product selection for maybe a whole week without taking a breath, but the short answer here is to go for the very niche area. So don't go for the mainstream products. Don't go for the current best sellers. Don't even go for the medium competition.

My strategy has always started with the very low competition products, every product I launch. There was one I launched last week. Already I'm on the top row of page one. I'm getting double figures of sales a day with not a single review. I'm not doing any give aways. I'm not doing any fancy rebates or tactical tricky stuff. Everything's completely organic and that's really healthy.

That means that when I get a sale, I know that people can find the product from particular keywords. I know that people are willing to pay full price. They won't just take it away because they're given some huge coupon discount code, and I know what they think of the product because the reviews that come through when they do come are real.

When you have no competition for your products, if you're a big fish in a small pond, life's a lot easy. You haven't got dodgy tactics. You don't have to bid hard for advertising. You get onto the top of page one really quickly, which is where the sales happen. You could have a way more popular product that is a kind of product there's a lot more volume every day. But if you're buried on page 62 and a half, nobody's ever going to find you.

Whereas a much more obscure product with a very unusual keyword or those keywords that describe the product that customers searched for, if that's pretty niche and obscure, then you'll be at the top of pageone with a good offering there.

And that's where you get a really high rate of sales and there are less customers, but more of those customers will buy from you. So Amazon loves those products. This helps them expand their range of products available for sale on their online category, on their catalogue. And you go into categories that aren't obvious and aren't where the other Amazon sellers are.

Question 6: Isn't Amazon saturated with sellers?

This is interesting, and I get this asked this question all the time.

As soon as I see I'm in a patch with lots of other professional Amazon sellers, I keep looking for another area or another product because I like to stay away from the competition. If I have to spend all my days fighting off the competition or promoting to get noticed or promoting to get the sale because the price is dropping from lots of competitors or being aggressive, then it's a race to the bottom.

But if I can spend my time adding more low competition but very high margin products, then I'm winning. I've got a passive income stream and I don't need to engage in all the aggressive marketing that you need on a more competitive product.

Question 7: So how do you find winning products to sell on Amazon?

So with lots of examples and case studies over the years, I've really figured out what criteria matter for products. And I've written for myself an eight-page product selection checklist that keeps me on the right tracks and thinking about the stuff that really matters with the new product is not just the supply and demand. It's also things like compliance or risk factors with the product: Even the practicalities of shipping, how it could be branded and how it could be part of a bigger brand. All of those factors need to be weighed up.

And there's never a perfect product, but I have to say I've never had a disaster with a product. The worst case I've ever had is that if it turns out to have been more competitive by the time I go live than when I did my research over a month or two, a bunch of new sellers also appeared and the price drops away, then I've just got out quickly and always been able to at least break even.

I've never lost money or had to pay to get rid of products or anything like that. But starting small and going low competition is definitely the strategy that's worked for me and worked for hundreds of my students as well.

Question 8: What software tool should I use?

Now for software that I recommend, there are lots of tools out there that promise a lot, and when I look at their numbers I sometimes wonder if they're absolutely accurate. And I also worry that everybody else is using the same software tools to pick the same products and they're all going to turn up and start selling them on the same day, which is a disaster. So I tend not to choose any of my products from the software.

I don't use it to recommend product ideas. So I follow my product selection strategy to find low competition, quite niche ideas for products.

And then I check out on Helium 10 how the numbers for that product look. So it saves me a bit of time rather than clicking through the whole category, looking at every listing, looking at the ranking, figuring out how many units a day, reading the reviews.

I like Helium 10 because it can summarize what's going on for that category or that keyword, who my competitors are going to be, what their fees are, what their volume is, what their sale price is, what their reviews say. So that's great. It saves me time, but it's not essential. If it disappeared tomorrow, my business wouldn't end and a lot of other people's would because that's the only way they know how to do business on Amazon.

It's very appealing because it's so simple and it sounds too good to be true. But often in business, the things that sound too good to be true might be.

You do need to do a little bit of online research of your own before you pick that product, both on Amazon and on Google and just sitting online and seeing what's going on with that category of products so that you only enter an area that's low competition and where there's profits to be made.

I like software for saving a bit of time, but it's not essential for anything that we do on Amazon. And I do think it's a bit of a red herring. It sounds so easy and simple. People can't resist it. But then I see loads of people turning up with the same products at once if they're too reliant on it.

So the strategy I teach is not reliant on software. It certainly helps cut down some time.

Question 9: What is your strategy for selling on Amazon, and building an Amazon business?

The Strategy I teach is not reliant on software. Certainly helps cut down some research time, but it's not the strategy for choosing the product. It's an interesting time because there's a lot slower rate of people leaving reviews. It's getting harder to get ranked. And if you're choosing a best selling product, there's some pretty tough competition.

There are a lot of factories in, say, China selling themselves. And so what that means for you, as a potential Amazon seller, is it's time to do Amazon like a real business. So this doesn't mean hiring a team, or an office, or all of the stuff a normal business or a franchise needs. There's no real overheads or change to the structure of the business, but just your way of thinking needs to be a little bit different.

You need to run your Amazon business like a real business. And build a brand where you're sourcing products that people have a reason to buy.

People see the quality or the point of difference, and they see a professionally presented listing, and they are compelled to buy. In the past you could get away with a very basic generic product and didn't really need to differentiate yourself to do very well. But now you need to go for lower competition products to get seen, because there's a lot of other low quality listings out there. And you need to go high-end premium priced, do a world-class job of the photography in the listing... And there's a best way to do that.

Which, after a few hundred products I've got quite fast and consistent at creating, and can show you how to as well. But really, it's not a time to be doing cheap generic products. It's time to go high-end premium and offer something to Amazon that they don't already have. So something with a bit of a point of difference, even if it's just nicer packaging or a free little gift. Something simple, but that just gives you a bit of an edge.

If you've got no edge, it's hard to compete just on price. You don't want to have to win a sale by being the cheapest. So, that's something I'm thinking about all the time.

How to be the best in a small category, rather than trying to be the cheapest in a big category? That's definitely the way this is trending. Now, the million-dollar question is, is there too much competition to get started on Amazon now?

I firmly believe that there's always money to be made on Amazon, both now and in the future. Online shopping is only going to grow. And I still see my products doing well, my students' products doing really well today. So I don't believe there is too much competition if you know which products to choose.

But if you choose the wrong products, something that's easy for your factory in China to make themselves, or something where there's already 10 pages of really great listings with lots of reviews. Then yes, that is a competitive area and wouldn't be a lot of fun.

Question 10: How and what should I launch for my first product?

Heading straight into a competitive niche or category is the worst place you can head as a new seller on Amazon. It looks comforting because you can see other people making money, but it's the worst place for you to try and launch your product in those crowded categories.

When you launch your first product make sure you go for something low competition, and low volume. Just enough to learn the ropes, get going, and see how nice those profits are when you're away from the mainstream products. And that's the strategy I use myself, and exactly the strategy I teach as well. So there's always somebody saying, "It's competitive." and "It was easier five years ago." But I think there's actually more opportunity than five years ago because there's even more people shopping on Amazon. It's growing so fast as a platform. And I'm really reassured by how the company's growing, and scaling, that this is the place where customers want to shop. And where I want to be selling, because people are only on Amazon to buy. All these other platforms are just tough.

And when people need to buy something they go to Amazon. Social media, they're just looking for input. Google, they're just doing research. They're not ready to load their credit card and spend money. Amazon is the place to be. It's where people spend money.

It's the most trusted brand in the United States. And some products are crowded for sure, but I see tons and tons of opportunity to do a different type of product to the mainstream Amazon sellers, and do extremely well, and generate lovely passive income streams.

Question 11: I hear drop shipping is the best Amazon strategy. Is that true?

So what's happening in the world of drop shipping? Well, there's a mixed bunch of things I have to say about drop shipping. Now the great thing is you don't need to buy as much stock up front. You've got the luxury of only having to pay your supplier when your customer has paid you. So that's great.

But you do also have to be pretty sharp on your Facebook advertising skills. So if you're driving people to your own website, then that's fine. Amazon doesn't really like drop shipping because they like products in their warehouse where they control the customer experience.

And if there's a delay, if the product arrives two weeks later from China after being sold on Amazon, that's not really the model Amazon's going for. They can't beat Alibaba or AliExpress at that game.

Amazon wins by being high quality products delivered with Amazon Prime. So free shipping for most customers, really fast shipping for all customers, if they choose it, and that's an advantage for customers that they really pay a premium for.

They trust Amazon, they know that their credit card is safe and that their order will arrive. If they're buying a gift, drop shipping's just so unreliable and slow. It's not going to usually do the job.

And people just love shopping on Amazon.

The range of products is all there under one roof. They've got their credit cards loaded, their delivery address loaded. They know it's secure. They know that what's in the image and in the description's exactly what's going to turn up.

They know Amazon's hard on people selling dodgy or low quality products. There's not going to be any counterfeits there. So people love Amazon as a shopping platform, and I love it as a selling platform.

And drop shipping has this one advantage of slightly better cash flow. But what you save in the products up front, you end up really having to spend on Facebook ads, or I'm hiring someone to do all the tracking and admin around, getting the products delivered to the customer.

Question 12: What are the advantages of Amazon's FBA (fulfilment by Amazon) model and private labelled products?

I'm a big fan of Amazon and the FBA model because it's all hands off. And any products I think that's good enough to sell I'd be willing... Based on my experience and following the right criteria, I'd then be more than willing to invest in a very small test run, launch order, and private label it from the beginning. So it's under my own brand.

It's very hard to... Well it's not hard, but it's easy to sell a drop shipping business. But you get a higher price for a Amazon brand that's got a private label because then you own the brand, you can control the price, and no one else can sell the product that's yours; compete on price. So drop shipping has got one little advantage.

But I think private labels have bigger strategic advantages overall around pricing, controlling your product and your supply chain, and controlling your business a lot more. So you can still make great money when you find these blue-sky products.

You can see Fiona here is just a relatively new seller. She's a student of mine, and she had a great day on Amazon Prime day in the middle of this year; so in July. So she really believes in this Amazon business model with FBA doing all the work.

She started out with about $3,000 and she's been investing in back into the business as she grows, and getting great results. And that's really changed her life. Fiona is actually a pharmacist. She had a great career. So switching away from that kind of career to look after her children and run her Amazon business. That's been a huge lifestyle change, and thanks to her Amazon product sales. So it does work. And this is really currently, these are people sourcing products in India, and China, and Vietnam, and all around the world, and getting going on Amazon, and seeing the difference it can make.

Question 13: What's the best way to get started?

If you'd like to get some personal coaching and become a student like Fiona, who's given up her day job, or like me, who's sold a business. Or just like lots of my students, who are generating a few extra thousand dollars a month, and it's really helping them live a better life. Then what you can do is click the link and book a no obligation Amazon fast track call with my all-star team. So they'll have a chat with you. They'll show you the best way to get started. Answer any questions you have. Explore what could be possible for you. And if you qualify, then there's a chance to get personal support from my team and I in finding those blue-sky products.

You might be looking to get going on Amazon, and we're looking for something to. We're looking for people who have at least a few thousand dollars to get started. This is a real business. You're going to need skills. You're going to need products. And this is just a drop in the ocean when you see what's possible later, but we want people who are realistic about making decisions to get going. So we really want consistent action takers. This isn't a get rich overnight scheme. This is a business that takes a few months to build up and build that portfolio of products. And we want people who are ready to go. We want to get you up and going soon. Started in the next 30 days selling, and maybe 90 days.

Question 14: What does a day in the life of a successful Amazon seller look like?

So most people this game says it's maybe four hours a week.

And I don't know if that's because Tim Ferriss wrote that great book (The 4-Hour Work week) but certainly I would spend a lot less than that on most of my Amazon businesses. In the beginning when you're doing product research for the first time, and learning how to get good at that, maybe a little bit more? So maybe on average an hour or so a day at the beginning, and then it would quickly tail off to be just minutes a day, and then just a few hours a week.

Maybe once a day you're checking your messages from Amazon, checking your sales look healthy. Once a week you're checking the key metrics, the sales looking good. The advertising costs are about right. Checking inventory levels in case something needs re-stocking, and maybe doing some more product research.

In the early days I was able to run my entire Amazon business as I commuted to work on the weekday morning. I had children at home and a day job still. And so for the first nine months I ran my business in about 20 minutes a day on the bus, and off my phone even; not even off a laptop. So once you know what you're looking for it really becomes a fairly simple and repetitive process. Rinse and repeat.

I also build a lot of cool lifestyle elements into my Amazon business. I travel a few times a year. I go to a couple of trade shows to go and look for products. Or I'll go and do trips to look for products overseas. So that's been really fun.

Sometimes my suppliers invited me to their countries; I was

invited to a wedding in Nepal by a supplier, and a wedding in China from another supplier. I went to a meet a supplier in Sri Lanka. So I've had some wonderful experiences in traveling through my Amazon business too.

But you can do the whole thing from home. And certainly for the first year I was still in the day job, and just fitting this into the little gaps around the side.

Keeping an eye on sales, sourcing new products, clearing the emails, just two or three a day maybe, and getting some quotes for new products. And once a week sitting down and progressing the best of those new product ideas.

So, none of it's hard when you know how. But you do need to invest a little bit of time at the start, maybe an hour or so a day, just to learn the strategies for the training and what you're looking for. And then get out there and find some winning products!

Question 14: What skills do I need to be a successful Amazon seller?[*]

I've just seen so many different people from different walks of life succeed on Amazon: students still at college, retirees and mums at home. I've seen people with a really solid IT background, and I've seen completely creative people who have no data, or kind of hard empirical kind of number data skills. They're real creative minds, and they find coming up with the product ideas, or the packaging kind of stuff, easy. And then they just learn how to ask the right questions of suppliers and double check the numbers carefully.

I've seen people who are very good project managers run it efficiently. And then I've seen people who were very inefficient

---

[*] Results not typical.

just follow a process, go step by step through, and they're up and selling before they know it. So there's no one particular skill that's essential. There's more of a temperament thing. It really suits people who just want to see the results. So if you've got a bit of motivation, or drive, to see some changes. That seems, I think, to be the biggest determinant of who's going to do well in this game. And there's people who are great academically, and people who've never done well, or even finished school, or had any further education.

So it's certainly not based on an education level. It's certainly not whether you're kind of right brain, left brain, or analytical, or creative. All those people can do well on Amazon. And I've seen all of them do well. But the main thing is just building confidence. And then all the skills you need you can easily learn, and they're not difficult. They're not advanced skills. It's just doing lots of little basics consistently, and then you get the result.

But a lot of my students, they're looking to make a few thousand dollars net profit per month that lets them choose to leave the day job. Choose to live a better lifestyle. Have a lot more free time. Live a healthier lifestyle. Do more of the stuff they're interested in, rather than spending their whole day working really hard for someone else.

The sky's the limit, and it's just all about what you're prepared to put into it. But certainly all the students I teach, I'm kind of trying to get them to think at the start. What will you do when this is successful? What does success look like?

Therefore, what kind of target monthly income do you need to aim for?

What monthly income do you need to aim for and how many products and what kind of size products are we looking for to make that happen for you?

So, you can work backwards, reverse engineer from any goal and make it happen. You can start small. You can aim to grow an empire from day one. It is totally up to you. It's not constrained by the platform. The only limit is your thinking.

Thank you for reading this and I hope answering these questions has given you a bit more insight as to how Amazon works, why I'm mad about the platform, and just think it's the best place to be and why so many people get such great results. There's so many things stacked up in your favor to become an Amazon seller and really change your situation for the better. Whatever it is you want to do, let's have I hope my team and I can help you.

FAST-START ONLINE MASTERCLASS

HOT SELLING AMAZON PRODUCTS
AND HOW TO FIND THEM

CLICK HERE TO REGISTER NOW

CHAPTER SEVEN

WHAT OTHER PEOPLE ARE SAYING ABOUT SOPHIE HOWARD*

Alex & Ayden - 'We really resonated with Sophie's Private Label Method, it felt authentic to us.'

We are about a little over a year into selling and we've just launched our first successful product which on track to replace, and even exceed, our current monthly income. We want a life of flexibility, we want a life of freedom, we want to spend our time with our family and traveling and having a job where we can work from anywhere in the world allows us that freedom.

We really resonated with Sophie's Private Label Method, it felt authentic to us. Ayden and I always knew that we wanted to start a business to serve other people we just didn't know

---

*   Results not typical. These stories are shared as examples of what some people have achieved with consistent effort and application. Amazon seller results vary depending on skill, background work ethic etc.

what and we didn't know how, and we felt like the private label method where we would be able to create our own brand with its own personality on Amazon's platform to showcase our products, to serve other people, felt the most like us.

We learned so much in just one year. We also have an amazing coach through Sophie's program. To anyone starting out we would just say have fun, try new things, don't be afraid to make mistakes, don't be afraid to learn from your mistakes and trust that the framework that you need is all laid out perfectly for you in Sophie's course.

Daniel - "...roughly two and a half months, we have brought in $8,200 in sales."

Hi, my name is Daniel. And I've had a career in web design and development for about 19 years. And I was really looking for a change. I came across Sophie's videos on YouTube about a year and a half ago. And as I was researching passive income ideas and Amazon FBA information, I was really looking for something to supplement my income and something that would be sort of a passive side hustle to begin with that could eventually turn into a full-time gig. And I really wanted this to replace my current career and something that didn't take up a lot of time so that I could free my time for my family and for things that I wanted to spend my time on.

I was really impressed with her approach, which is why I ended up taking the course. She really has a different approach to a lot of the other Amazon courses that I looked at. And she's really down to earth. And what she presents through the course is really realistic and makes a lot of business sense as well.

In the past, I tried to make money online in lots of different ways and didn't find actually very much success in that. And I always put that down to it being too competitive or too saturated. And particularly on Amazon, I've always felt that. But what Sophie presents through the course actually really is inspiring. Because it doesn't matter in the way that she approaches it. It doesn't matter if it's too saturated or if there's a lot of competition overall. Because you're looking for gaps in the market. You're looking for ways that you can differentiate yourself and your products and fill those gaps in the market and create strong brand and strong products. And something that really works well on Amazon.

My wife and I have been through the course and through the process and we've actually just launched two private label products. We've created a brand and they went online on Amazon in November 2019. So roughly two and a half months, we have brought in $8,200 in sales. And we have a really healthy profit margin as well at 55%.

So we're super pleased with the results. Things are going fantastic. It's growing every day and things are looking just as we had imagined they would and how we planned for. And that is largely down to the methodology that Sophie teaches.

It's been a really challenging time. We've learned a ton. And there's a ton of details and things that you've got to really experience to know. But Sophie's course covers that. The Facebook community that is really strong and helpful. And if you ever have any questions, they're always there to answer. There's private coaching sessions, which have been tremendous, and just to learn from really experienced sellers.

I would definitely highly recommend this course to anyone regardless of your experience, whether you're just the beginner or you have sales experience online, or even Amazon experiences. There's a lot to be gleaned from this course. And particularly with the coaching sessions, just a lot of value there. And it's worked really well for us. So I highly recommend it.

Gwen - "...product is currently bringing in 1,300 net on average per month. It may not seem huge, but that's definitely in line with my strategy."

Hi, my name's Gwen and I live in Auckland, New Zealand. I'm CEO of a charity, and I'm originally from Manchester in the UK.

Now I've been Googling dropshipping, how to publish an ebook, other ways of generating an income online. So of course, Facebook stalked me, and I got sent a whole world of promo videos for Amazon, including Sophie's Blue Sky promo.

What made Sophie stand out from all the others was a couple of things. Firstly, the bulk, and I appreciate this … This is a generalization, but the bulk of people presenting these courses are young, American and male. I'm none of those things. So it's perhaps not surprising that Sophie actually really resonated with me personally. And I thought, if Sophie can achieve that success in Amazon, then actually, so can I, and that felt really reassuring.

What I also liked about Sophie's presentation was the fact that it was really let's get to the point, no nonsense. For me, that's really important. And I also loved the fact that she was promoting niche and private labeling, which is the opposite to the majority of courses out there. So that's what made me sign up.

Now, as I said, I work for a charity and it is amazing. It's just such a privilege to be able to do that. However, it is such, such hard work in a really competitive marketplace. I always do a massive eye roll every time somebody says to me, and it happens quite a lot, every time somebody says to me, "Gwen, when I'm getting to retirement, I'm going to slow down a bit and I'm going to do some charity work too." It is hard work. It's like working for any other company. The only difference is that the profits do amazing things, and I love that.

But what I want going forward, and the reason that I signed up for this course, is that I still want to do good, but I want to do good on my own terms. Now, I'm 47, going to be 50 in three years' time, that's my goal for being my own employer, working for myself, working part-time, having the opportunity to do more travel, particularly around this beautiful country that I am privileged to live in. So I really want to be able to do that.

Now, for my first product on Amazon, I've really taken a niche thing on board, and it's a fundraising product, which is an area I know really, really well and I'm really passionate about. It's a product that is selling to churches, a lot of churches, actually, companies, gyms, schools, colleges, sports groups, Scouts,

Guides. So the whole world of people who could actually buy this product.

What I've done is I've also developed an online presence through Facebook and my own website, which provides fundraising coaching. And I've managed to dovetail the two so when somebody buys my product, they also get an ebook and they get an invitation to join my online community, so it's a product with real benefits around it. It certainly stands out in terms of the product page and it is right up there on page one and has been pretty much from day one.

That product is currently bringing in 1,300 net on average per month. It may not seem huge, but that's definitely in line with my strategy. I'm currently in the process developing three more products. Whilst they're in the pipeline, my first product is due to land any moment now in Canada and in the UK, and I'm really confident on my projections that that first product across the three markets will net me 2,500 per month. My goal for this brand is 10,000 net per month, and I believe I'll be able to achieve that with my next three products plus my first one across the markets. So I'm really, really pleased with that.

It's given me the confidence to think bigger. So what I'm going to do now, now that I've learned the ropes through Sophie, through the brilliant support and advice within the Facebook group ... And actually, I love the fact that I'm now in a position to be able to give advice and support. Isn't that great, that we can really help each other like that? Anyway, I digress.

Kirstin - "...just a few weeks into having all those products, but I'm already sort of selling between 10 and 20 units a day. And that's making about between 300 and 600 US dollars a day"

Hello, I'm Kirstin. I am in the UK. I am fairly new to the Amazon world. I come from a hospitality background. I've recently sold the hospitality business. I worked in that trade for 20 odd years, so I was looking for something where I didn't have to work every hour under the sun.

I wanted something with a much better work-life balance. I came across the Amazon opportunity on Facebook and it really appealed to me because I could choose my own hours, work from home. If I didn't want to, I didn't have to hire staff and deal with all the stress that that brings or deal with customers all day long. So that's what really appealed to me.

At first I thought I would be able to do it on my own. I thought I'd be able to find the information I needed to sort of learn what I needed to learn, but the more I got into it, the more I realized that I needed some help and I needed some advice from someone that was doing it the right way that knew what they were talking about.

There's lots of gurus out there and experts, but I wanted to learn the right way and that's what attracted me to Sophie's course. She just seemed genuine right from the off. And I really liked the structure of the course with the coaches and having the one-on-one time with coaches and being part of a community where I can interact with other students. So I wasn't doing it all on my own. And I'm really glad that I did choose Sophie's course because I've only been sort of selling for a couple of months, but I already know the way my products are going, that I've done things the right way and that I've learned the right way using the methods that Sophie teaches. My first product went live a couple of months ago and three weeks ago I launched another nine products.

So, just a few weeks into having all those products, but I'm already sort of selling between 10 and 20 units a day. And that's making about between 300 and 600 US dollars a day. So it's still early days, but I'm really pleased with how it's going so far. One of the best bits for me is while I put all the hard work in, I go to bed, and my product sell while I'm asleep. So I wake up and check my account to see how many of my products have sold, which is so different from my hospitality life. Probably the most important thing for me on a personal level is I've recently lost a very special family member and because I now work from home, the last couple of months, I've been able to spend caring for that family member, spending time.

And I got to be there at the very end when it really mattered. So, sales figures and numbers and everything is all wonderful, but at the end of the day, it's time with loved ones that is the most precious for me anyway. And so I'm really grateful that I've been able to do that because had I still been in my old life in hospitality or most any other nine to five job, I wouldn't have been able to take that time, that precious time.

So for anyone that's considering doing Sophie's course, just do it. You'll learn so much. You'll be so grateful. You got to put the hard work in, but you have so much support around you. In an industry that is a little bit lonely sometimes, just you and your computer screen, I really don't feel alone because I have my... The one on one time with coaches and the community around you and you get to know the other students and you can have as much interaction with them as you want to. So it really is a great community with a lot of support there if you need it. So just do it. You won't regret it. Best of luck.

Lucy - "...happy to find that I was instantly on page one and instantly making sales."

Hi guys. My name's Lucy, I'm a remedial massage therapist here in Melbourne. I'm a mum with three kids, and I work from home most of the time. So I was looking for some way to find a bit of, I guess, a bit of a side hustle that would help assist me in having that full time income, but not actually sacrificing my time in order to find that balance between my kids and my work life.

So, yeah, so I went looking for a course or some avenue that would help satisfy that criteria and considered selling on Amazon for a long time, actually, for several years, but didn't actually know which steps to take, how to do it. It was quite overwhelming and intimidating. However, I was quite savvy as far as finding out what side hustles would suit me and my lifestyle. I went on a trip to Guatemala, May 2019, and found a fantastic supplier of products there for a women's cooperative that really worked in line with my values.

So what I wanted to do was then find a way that I could help these women and support them as well through their community and raising their children. These are women who have experienced hardship and have very minimal employment opportunities. So I thought Amazon would be a good platform for me to be able to assist them and also help me balance my lifestyle a bit better as well. When I was looking for an Amazon course, I came across Sophie's course and liked her approach because she was very relatable and also had similar values to me as far as managing children but not wanting to sacrifice too much time with the children, and live, I guess, a different sort of lifestyle. So as I found Sophie so relatable, I decided to sign up for her course.

Before having done the course, the challenges that I came up against was how to find a product that would actually sell on Amazon instead of going in blindly. So how do you actually do the research and know that you're not just going to spend thousands of dollars on a product and then end up losing a lot of money because you haven't done your due diligence and don't know what you're up against as far as competitors go? So, and also how to find suppliers, ethical... Well, not ethical suppliers necessarily, but suppliers who are going to do the right thing by you, I guess. Anyway, so I found Sophie and as a result of doing the course was able to understand the process really clearly through the step by step modules and the assistance of the coaches. So after spending a few months doing all that research and finding out what is going to actually work, I applied what I learnt and found a product that I felt was going to work well.

So I took the plunge and actually got the product up and running, and I got it in quarter four. So I managed to get the product in about three months ago at... halfway through quarter four, and was very, very happy to find that I was instantly

on page one and instantly making sales. So that was a huge success for me. And it continued to do more sales. So I realized that the product, my first product, was actually seasonal, so a seasonal product. So now I'm working on increasing my product base to non-seasonal products. So products that will sell all year round. And I'm thrilled to say that I am now an active supporter of these this women's cooperative in Guatemala, helping them to sustain financial independence and improve their quality of life and the quality of life of those people within that community. So if you are considering doing the Amazon course, I would highly recommend working with Sophie because she works with integrity and her coaches offer you full support. And I couldn't be happier with the results from doing the course. So thank you and all the best, good luck.

Peter - "What's helped me throughout the course? Perseverance I think, learning perseverance is a key."

Hi there. My name's Peter Judd, I'm based in Auckland, New Zealand. I'm involved in the training industry at the moment. I saw Sophie's advertisement online.

I was looking for a business that would not be hours based. In other words, it would work when I wasn't. Also, I wanted to have something that would be locationally independent, I could work from anywhere. The other thing I suppose too, is that I didn't want something that would require a formal certification. I mean, it's a bit late for me to be a doctor or a welder or something. I just really wanted to have a business that I could run with. The other thing as far as looking at other training courses go, I did look at a number of others and I felt that Sophie's overall was more down to earth. I felt that it was headless hype and I felt that in a word it was genuine and that's proved to be the case.

I launched my first product in December 2019, so it's been a couple of months. I've sold a few products, but I'm not satisfied yet. There was a lot more to come, it's a work in progress, but I had started. I guess the big change that occurred with me was the new language. I mean, what the heck is PPC? What's private labeling? What's FBA? All these different things. How do I find a product? How do I know if it's going to be viable or not? Why am I selling this product, why am I pursuing it? What's the problem that I'm trying to solve in selling this product?

What's helped me throughout the course? Perseverance I think, learning perseverance is a key. Stories from others, it really helped as well. The coaching sessions are really valuable, in fact, they're essential. And also most importantly for me personally, it was a track to run on, I need a track to run on. The main difference that that's made for me overall is an awareness that I can be part of something that actually works as a business. And if you're considering joining Sophie's training course, I'd recommend that you check out the other ones first, put the dipstick in, put the feelers out and make sure this one's for you. And if it is, jump in boots and all, and give it a hundred percent. All the very best with your business.

BONUS CHAPTER EIGHT

SELLING AN AMAZON BUSINESS FOR A BIG POTENTIAL PAYDAY

How to Build an Amazon Business to Sell

Please note, this is general education only, based on my experience in selling Amazon businesses. For personal financial advice on selling your Amazon business, please see an qualified accountant or Business broker who specializes in the area.

I've now sold 2 Amazon businesses, and it's really my #1 wealth strategy.

Build an Amazon business. Enjoy the cashflow. Then sell it for a lump sum to pay down mortgages or invest in real estate. And then rinse and repeat.

Because, when you know how to find profitable Amazon products…the skies the limit!

Keep the following in mind when starting an Amazon business that you plan to sell.

The first goal beyond picking a niche and great product is to be generating over 100K in net profit and under five million. That is the sweet spot.

You want to make your selection of products difficult to copy as this will be one of the first objections to assessing an Amazon business with longevity in mind.

Factors for building a saleable business:

- Really good brand or brands
- Good prospectus written
- Products with categories that are ungated
- Perfect metrics
- Plenty of stock but not too much
- Agreements in place with all suppliers
- Confidentiality Agreements with Virtual Assistants
- Design files that are all in one place

When deciding to take on your business, a broker will want to see:

- Uniqueness of products, ideally diversified across a large number products
- Solid supply chain
- Profit margins of up to 20%+
- Market share

- Systems that are in place
- Team who run the business
- Number of products

In order to pitch your business to prospective buyers, a business broker will need answers to the following:

- Why should someone buy this?
- What is the story behind the brand?
- What will make it hard for people to copy the brand and the products?
- What percentage of the products are consumables?
- Are there trademarks and patents in place?

Who comes with the business, for example which team members and or will the founder be able to offer monthly consulting hours for a 'smooth hand over'.

When a prospective buyer of your business undertakes their due diligence, here is a list of what they will require:

- Sales reports
- Bank statements
- Login to your Amazon Account
- Agreements that you have in place

- Accounting financials to track numbers
- Collateral such as marketing and systems

The key to making the process easy is to enable transparency by keeping a very ordered and organized set of financials, agreements and filing systems.

You will need to be able to prove what you claim in the prospectus (such as profit and loss numbers) and make the process as easy as possible.

The broker will value an Amazon products business usually with a net profit multiple of two and in some cases three.

This means for example, if you have a $30,000 USD per month profit business, you could sell for as much as $1 million USD.

You will need to have been in business for at least a year and safely for 18 months. You will need to prove that you have a diversity of products with revenue that is growing steadily. A seasonal business is fine but spiky revenue will not be adequate.

You need to show a spread of risk with hundreds of products, not necessarily all selling in large quantities, and it is ok to have variations of the same product. Businesses that are based on few products are more risky.

The less cash you take out of the business the better. This will be more attractive for the buyer as they will have a business with available cash to use straight away.

If you are selling to a US buyer they will want to see tax returns. Generally, what you are selling is the account only and not the company. You will need to take the paperwork side of the business very seriously.

The buyer will want to see:

- 18 months profit
- Monthly stock take reports
- Profit and loss
- Balance sheet
- Current and up to date cash flow
- Bills paid up

Once you get the valuation done, you add inventory after that.

For Amazon businesses that are earning up towards three million to five million the buyer would tend to be a private equity group. Below that, and the buyer will tend to be an individual.

When working with a broker you want to make sure that they eliminate prospects that have no real intention of buying the business.

Good brokers will get a letter of intent to buy the business from the buyer, once the due diligence process is completed.

They will also obtain signed confidentiality agreements and can even go as far as checking the potential buyers bank account to verify that they have the money to buy the business.

This avoids prospects snooping around to obtain private and confidential information about good product niches and financials.

Quarter one is a very good time to list an Amazon business for sale. This is because most people do their shopping heading into Chinese New Year. When Chinese New Year hits all suppliers are closed and people have more time on their hands.

Thank you so much for reading my book 'Amazon Boom'.

I hope you got some good ideas from it, and you are now ready to take action!

I wish you every success in your Amazon journey.

Sophie Howard

FAST-START ONLINE MASTERCLASS

HOT SELLING AMAZON PRODUCTS
AND HOW TO FIND THEM

CLICK HERE TO REGISTER NOW

Exercise 5:

If we were talking in 12 months, what results would you like to have achieved in your Amazon business to feel satisfied and happy with your progress?

_____

_____

_____

_____

_____

_____

_____

End

Made in the USA
Middletown, DE
20 November 2020